THE WRITE HELP

Resources and Activities for Word Processing

THE WRITE HELP

Resources and Activities for Word Processing

Grades 4-8

Ideal for Apple II users and easily adapted for other software and computers

Hugh Mehan	Randall Souviney
Barbara Miller-Souviney	Kim Whooley
Margaret Riel	Bea Liner

Scott, Foresman and Company

Glenview, Illinois   London

MORE GOOD YEAR BOOKS® IN COMPUTER EDUCATION

BYTE-SIZED ACTIVITIES
The Generic Word Processing Book
Grades 4-8
Thomas E. Boudrot

LOGO FOR TEACHERS
A Hands-On Approach
Grades K-6
Richard Howell, Patrick Scott, and Jean Rachowski

MASTERING THE MICRO
Using the Microcomputer in the Elementary Classroom
Grades K-6
Dorothy H. Judd and Robert C. Judd

For information about these or any Good Year Books®, please contact your local school supply store or

Good Year Books
Scott, Foresman and Company
1900 East Lake Avenue
Glenview, IL 60025

ISBN 0-673-18289-4

1 2 3 4 5 6—MAL—90 89 88 87 86 85

Contents

6

7

8

Introduction

The language arts activities presented here are designed for use with microcomputers in elementary and junior high school classrooms. Although the scheduled time listed for each activity assumes that students have full-time access to one computer with a disk drive and a printer, teachers have used the activities successfully in situations where a computer is available for only part of the school year as well as in computer laboratories with 12 to 15 computers available. Of course, the amount of instruction time actually required will depend on the grade level and the amount and frequency of computer use by each student.

Organization

The Write Help is organized into eight chapters. The first chapter reviews the current use of microcomputers in schools and identifies problems that arise out of the prevailing emphasis on drill and practice and programming. The second chapter presents the framework for an alternative approach, one that treats the microcomputer as a tool to assist teachers in meeting the educational goals in the language arts area. In order to integrate microcomputers with language arts instruction, *The Write Help* emphasizes a holistic instructional approach and procedures which exploit the interactive capabilities of microcomputers. The third chapter—which serves as a transition between the general theoretical framework for computer use in schools found in the preceding chapters and the specific language arts activities that follow—covers the role of the teacher in computer software development and relates the use of computers to the writing process. It also includes a short section for novice teachers on the parts of a microcomputer and how they work.

Chapters 4-8 present five sets of computer activities ready for classroom use. After a brief overview of classroom management issues, Chapter 4 offers a set of activities ("Introducing The Classroom Computer") designed to introduce students to basic computer operations and keyboarding skills. Chapter 5 introduces the use of the word processor for writing, and Chapters 6, 7, and 8 offer structured writing experiences for poetry, expository writing, and developing a class or school newspaper. Appendices include a list of software and source books for teachers; a glossary; and blackline masters of task cards, posters, and overhead projector slides.

Each activity in Chapters 4-8 begins with an instructional objective. Written as a guide to the teacher and not intended to specify performance criteria, each objective can be adapted to meet a range of student needs by selecting appropriate content and adjusting the complexity of the writing tasks involved.

Field-Tested Materials

The materials in this book are the result of research and development conducted under the auspices of teachers in the Oceanside Unified School District and the Vista Unified School District in collaboration with researchers from the University of California, San Diego. Field testing took place in grade 4-8 classrooms with diverse student populations—i.e., students came from different socioeconomic and ethnic backgrounds. Student abilities measured from the lowest CTBS quartile to those with Gifted and Talented Education (GATE) qualifications.

By observing and participating in the field testing of these materials in various classrooms, the authors gained valuable knowledge about ways to organize classrooms for instruction with computers, patterns of teacher-student interaction, and modes of student learning.

Actual Vs. Generic Software and Hardware

To aid the teacher who is relatively new to using a computer in the classroom, the authors chose to employ descriptions of actual software and the Apple computer rather than attempt to write generic descriptions of word processing software. The examples and activities throughout the book utilize *The Writer's Assistant* word processor (requires one disk drive) and a series of *Interactive Writing Tools* (Encyclopaedia Britannica Educational Corporation). These software products exemplify the approach to teaching writing advocated in Chapters 1-3.

The Writer's Assistant is also the editor in the *QUILL* program (D.C. Heath). *QUILL* (requires two disk drives) also offers several unique features which can facilitate children's writing. Several of the popular microcomputers and word processing systems designed for the novice writer (e.g., *The Bank Street Writer*) can be substituted in activities requiring text editing. Alternatives to the *Interactive Writing Tools* software are suggested where appropriate, and the annotated list of writing software products at the back of *The Write Help* provides further information.

Acknowledgments

A grant from the California State Department of Education, Educational Technology Local Assistance Program, supported the research and development upon which this book is based. The authors gratefully acknowledge this support.

They also acknowledge the support of Dr. Gary Olson, Superintendent of the Vista Unified School District, and Dr. Steven Speach, Superintendent of the Oceanside Unified School District. Principals Raub Mathias of Olive School, Eloise Wise of Palmquist School, Timothy Keane of Garrison School, and the staff at each school also deserve thanks for their patience and understanding.

The authors owe a debt of gratitude to James Levin for his efforts in designing much of the software discussed in *The Write Help* and to Robert Rowe for his pioneering utilization of word processing in his classroom. Their work has significantly influenced the ideas presented in this book. Finally, the authors wish to thank Marcia Boruta, Christy Drale, Moshe Cohen, Luis Moll, and Marti Tum Suden—all of whom made many valuable suggestions on early drafts of the manuscript—and Norma Allison for her patient efforts on the word processor to make this material presentable.

It is the hope of everyone associated with *The Write Help* that the ideas presented in this book will help teachers better integrate writing and computers in their daily instruction.

The Current State of Microcomputer Use in Schools

We frequently hear that we are in the midst of a "computer revolution." Virtually every scholarly report that discusses computers invokes the "revolution" metaphor. The popular press reinforces this view of the revolutionary role computers are playing in education, business, and home life. In 1984, *Time Magazine* selected the microcomputer as its "Man of the Year."

Although this book describes uses of computers in classrooms—and hence would seem to be a participant in the revolution—we want to take a critical look at the notion that computers can contribute to a revolution in education. In order to justify the claim that such a revolution is occurring, there must be evidence of significant changes in the social organization of schools, the way in which instruction takes place in classrooms, and the very knowledge that students are acquiring.

A Computer Revolution in Education?

The issue is not whether computers are present in schools or whether they are being used in classrooms. Computers *are* present in schools (their numbers are increasing), and they *are being used* in classrooms.

By Hugh Mehan

Classroom use of the microcomputer, however, is largely restricted to drill and practice. A classic example of "old wine in new bottles," classroom computers are being used as high-tech teaching machines: new devices meeting traditional educational goals. From our point of view, a computer revolution in education must involve the use of computers in new ways to achieve important educational goals—goals that could not be readily achieved without computers—or to achieve entirely new educational objectives.

Previous Attempts at Innovation in Education. This is not the first time that a significant innovation has been introduced into schools. An examination of previous attempts to make changes in schools provides a framework for understanding the "revolution" in education associated with the advent of microcomputers.

Among the efforts to change schools by introducing new technology or curricula are the "new math," inquiry learning in science, "open classrooms," and the Experimental Schools Program. Most of these efforts have met with limited success. Sarason (1982) described limited success as:

1. The program of change did not last longer than outside funding or support;

2. There was no discernible impact on the organization of education within the school.

Why were the efforts to change schools so transient? One reason involves the origins of the recommendations. The proponents of curricula change and removal of classroom walls most often came from outside the school system—i.e., people in universities, corporations, and foundations. The people working within the school culture seldom shared the enthusiasm of the "external" reformers for these changes. Throughout the accounts of failed attempts to innovate runs a recurrent theme: Attempts to introduce change that emanate from outside the school system are not highly successful. Externally imposed approaches have not been successful because they fail to take into account the effects the changes have on the full range of activities within the school.

A second reason these innovations have not had a significant impact on the organization of instruction is that proponents assumed that change could be achieved without shifting the regular patterns of action in schools. They did not seem to realize that altering the techniques of teaching science or mathematics would produce a concurrent impact on virtually every other aspect of the school. Although new math and science curricula were developed, tested, and revised, no consideration was given to the relationship between those curricula and other subjects. Likewise, the relationship among the teachers of new math and science, other faculty, and the administrative structure of the schools was not taken into account. Instead, the agents of change adopted an engineering approach to solving problems of poor math and science instruction, school governance, and the ecology of the school. This approach failed to relate proposed changes to their impact on other aspects of the school system's operation.

A third possible reason for the failure to implement these changes concerns the scope of the recommendations. Reformers such as Conant (1959), Silberman (1970), and Goodlad (1984) all focused on the organization of schools; none examined the relationship between the school and the wider society. In their assessments, the reformers seldom included the social and economic conditions of the communities and society surrounding the schools. History has shown that failing to take into account race relations, community politics, and stratified economic opportunities when considering changes in the organization of schooling dooms the success of innovations.

The Introduction of Computers into Schools.   In general, these unsuccessful attempts to introduce change were introduced by people at the top of the educational system rather than by people indigenous to the culture of the school. The process by which computers are being introduced, however, is different in many respects from previous attempts at innovation.

Sheingold et al. (1983) and Allan (1984) point out that the introduction of computers into schools is primarily a grass roots phenomenon. Teachers, not high-ranking administrators or outside agencies interested in change, have been bringing computers into schools. The first teachers to become involved with microcomputers did so on their own time. Mostly self taught, they learned more and more about computers through personal interest. They acquired microcomputers and enrolled in courses of computer study at their own expense. Eventually, they began teaching students to program, solve problems, and use text editors. As knowledge of their expertise became more widely known, they started teaching colleagues—informally at first, then under institutional sponsorship: district or county sponsored inservice workshops and university extension programs. Some even approached neighborhood computer stores and requested free or inexpensive software and hardware for use in their classrooms. Teachers have been the driving force behind the introduction and spread of computers in schools.

Parents have pressured school districts to offer courses on computing and to include computers in the school curriculum. Whether motivated by the fear that their children would not develop the necessary skills to compete for jobs or influenced by advertising claims that every home must have a computer, parents have become involved in the process of introducing computers into schools to a greater degree than they participated in the many previous attempts to introduce change in schools.

Computer companies, interested in selling their products, also have played a role in the process. Perhaps believing that students familiar with computers in school will urge their parents to purchase computers for home, Apple, Kaypro, Hewlett-Packard and other computer companies have donated computers to schools. In California, legislation provides tax breaks for companies donating computer hardware, and industry give-away programs are being considered in several other states as well.

Innovative teachers, motivated parents, and aggressive business interests constitute a coalition for change that is unique in educational history. It is a coalition that operates more closely to the bottom of the school hierarchy than to the top.

Prevailing Uses of the Microcomputer

Having considered some of the characteristics of previous attempts to change schools, we will now examine some ways in which microcomputers are currently being used in schools.

Recent national surveys of computer use (CSOS, 1983; Tucker, 1983) and regional surveys (e.g., in the San Diego area: Miller, 1983; Boruta et al., 1983; Cohen, 1984) have shown that the current state of computer use in schools presents educators and society at large with a number of problems. First, because microcomputers are used largely to provide drill and practice in basic skills, schools are not fully utilizing the capabilities of computer technology for education. Second, some students—women and those from lower income and ethnic minority groups—do not have the same access to educational technology as do their male, middle income, nonminority counterparts. Third, treating computer programming as the pinnacle of a computer curriculum overlooks the needs of society and the workplace.

Basic Skills Instruction. Basic skills instruction, the prevailing use of classroom computers today, usually means "Computer Aided Instruction"—or CAI (*see* Atkinson, 1972; Suppes, 1980). A recent study (Patterson, 1983) indicates the extent to which CAI software is used. Two thousand computer-using teachers were asked: "What are your favorite educational software programs?" Of the 93 programs identified, 27 were for professional and administrative purposes and 66 were for instructional purposes. Nearly all of the instructional programs, however, were devoted to drill and practice or reinforcement of existing skills in math, social science, and English. They were not used to generate new instructional activities.

Programs designed for basic skills instruction commonly give students drill and practice on material already presented in their classrooms. The material to be learned and the sequence in which it is learned are rigidly fixed by the teacher and the software. The material is restricted to a specific problem domain, offers a narrow range of response options, and is presented in very small steps (Amarel, 1983; Riel, 1983). When students select a correct answer, they are rewarded with a visual or musical display, often unrelated to lesson materials.

Programming. The second most common instructional application of computers in schools is intended to promote "computer literacy"—i.e., teaching students to program, primarily in the BASIC language.

Programming is emphasized because it enables students to gain control of the machine (Papert, 1980). Some claim that programming also strengthens students' higher level reasoning skills, but there is little evidence to support such a contention. Even if the evidence did exist, teaching all students to program in BASIC would seem to be shortsighted.

BASIC is a general-purpose programming language. While its linear structure makes it relatively easy to learn initial commands and statements, this same structure makes BASIC difficult for beginning students to create any but the most rudimentary programs. BASIC is also limited in that it does not easily allow for hierarchically arranged programming procedures as do the more modern languages of Pascal and Logo.

Whether working in BASIC, Pascal, or Logo, however, students receive only a limited sense of the computer's power. With special-purpose languages such as Interactive Texts or spread sheets, students develop a richer sense of how to structure problems effectively and how to approach problems in a disciplined way, two of the general skills that some cognitive scientists believe can be widely applied when solving problems.

Problems With Current Uses of Microcomputers

A number of problems exist regarding the ways microcomputers are used in schools. In addition to the failure to capitalize on the full capabilities of computer technology, schools tend to stratify access to microcomputers along gender, social class, and ethnic lines. Of equal importance, schools are not using computers in ways that match the ways computers are used in the workplace.

Underutilization of the Computer's Capabilities. The fast pace and packaged format of CAI drill and practice software provide students with little opportunity to deliberate, reconsider, or challenge prespecified answers. These programs assume limited knowledge and aim to strengthen and broaden that knowledge through repeated exposure to a similar class of exercises (Amarel, 1983). They make little attempt, however, to extend or apply existing knowledge.

While some evidence exists suggesting that microcomputers can deliver basic skills instruction better than conventional techniques (Kulik et al., 1983), critics of such studies (Tucker, 1983) point to the methodological problems and cost-comparison omissions. Typically, the effectiveness studies compare the effects of recently introduced CAI programs to conventional workbook activities, comparisons that may provide a statistically significant

advantage for CAI. So far, however, effectiveness studies have not compared CAI to cross-age tutoring and other methods which also have been shown to improve students' learning. Moreover, when the high cost of computers is taken into account, the advantage of CAI over conventional techniques for improving students' basic skills is diminished.

Furthermore, CAI workbook pages lack the motivating effect required to sustain student interest once the novelty of working with computers has worn off (Malone, 1981). In addition, the readability and graphic quality of those electronic worksheets currently available are poorer than printed workbook pages, making their use as an alternative methodology questionable.

Equitable Access to Educational Technology. Access to classroom computers and the uses to which those computers are put differ across social, racial, and income lines. Ethnic minority and low income students receive a different kind of instruction on computers than do their nonminority, middle income contemporaries. While middle class students—especially those who are in advanced programs (e.g., Gifted and Talented Education)—receive instruction which encourages learner initiative in areas such as programming and problem solving, low income and ethnic minority students receive CAI instruction which maintains the control of learning within the program (CSOS, 1983; Boruta et al., 1983).

Although males and females have equal access to computers in elementary schools that have established central computer labs, this equality disappears in secondary schools (CSOS, 1983; Boruta et al., 1983; Sheingold et al., 1983). Even in elementary schools, more boys than girls use computers in their spare time (recess, lunch, after-school clubs). Moreover, when students are divided into curricular tracks (college preparatory, vocational, and general education) in secondary schools, a stratification of males and females becomes apparent, with the males gaining greater access to computer and math labs.

This tracking of students by gender and socioeconomic background through different curricular tracks stratifies students' access to information technology. Differential access represents one of the ways in which the microcomputer can contribute to the further stratification of our society. If only a few people learn to control computers while the majority can only react passively to them, then we will have a system of stratification based on access to information technology (Schiller, 1981) that will make class systems based on economic differences (Marx, 1964) and cultural differences (Bourdieu and Passeron, 1977; Collins, 1980) pale by comparison.

The Needs of Society and the Workplace. The computer is a general-purpose machine. It processes information that can be used for a wide variety of instructional and administrative purposes. These wide-ranging capabilities, coupled with pressure from parents and business interests, are the main reasons computers are having such a dominant impact on education.

Knowing that the computer *can* be used for almost any purpose does not inform schools about how it should be used. In fact, it is its flexibility that is so dazzling. Since the machine can be programmed to do so many things, we must search for the constraints which tell us which computer applications make sense and which do not. This search must also take into consideration the cost of applications in dollars, time, and human effort.

As schools and universities organize educational curricula involving computers, we need to insure that the instruction students receive will help them in the world of work. It is helpful, therefore, to examine the ways in which computers presently function in the workplace and to try to predict how computers will be used at work in the future.

Most computer scientists believe that within a few years only a small number of people will actually be writing programs with general-purpose languages. Right now, microcomputers are being used for word processing, spread-sheet analysis, and data management—applications which do not require knowledge of general-purpose computer languages. Those who use computers for such applications are not highly skilled programmers but rather employees who learn how to create electronic forms and spread sheets provided by special-purpose, user-friendly programs (e.g., *Apple Works, Sensible Speller, MousePaint*). Eventually, computers will write programs in response to typed or even spoken requests made in ordinary English (Kay, 1983), further reducing the need for a multitude of general language programmers.

The shift in computer uses from those dependent upon general-purpose programming languages to those using special-purpose programs suggests that even though our society may rely heavily on the computer, we will not need a vast number of programmers. And while a shortage of general-purpose programmers currently exists, we are likely to need far fewer in the future.

The available evidence suggests that most jobs will *not* be found in high-technology industries and that the presence of such technology in the workplace will *not* require a vast upgrading of the American labor force (Levin and Rumberger, 1983). On the contrary, the proliferation of high technology is far more likely to reduce the skill requirements of American workers than to upgrade them.

Levin and Rumberger (1983) cite Labor Department projections that say jobs for computer programmers will grow between 74 and 148 percent during the 1980s in comparison with an overall job growth of just 22 percent. These percentages are misleading, however. The *total* number of new jobs for computer programmers is expected to be 150,000, while some 1.3 million new jobs are projected for janitors, nurses aides, and orderlies. In other words, nine new unskilled jobs will be available for every new job in computer programming. Similarly, new jobs for data processing machine mechanics—the fastest growing job category—will increase 148 percent, but that large gain translates into an increase of fewer than 100,000 new jobs. By comparison, 800,000 new jobs are projected for fast-food workers and kitchen helpers.

There will be neither a proliferation of systems analyst jobs, nor will high-tech jobs create demands for increasingly sophisticated work skills. On the contrary, microcomputers—by simplifying routine tasks and reducing the opportunities for worker individuality and judgment—will make it possible to employ persons with lower skills to perform what had previously been highly sophisticated jobs in such diverse areas as office administration, data processing, drafting, and wholesale and retail trade.

This brief examination of computer uses in the world of work has implications for the widespread teaching of programming in the classroom. Strictly on intellectual and academic grounds, it may be important for students to gain some exposure to programming. Indeed, programming may enable students to gain a sense of how the computer operates and to develop skills in structuring problems. Devoting years to programming instruction, however, cannot be justified on the grounds that students will require such skills in the workplace (Tucker, 1983). We may need tens of thousands of general-purpose programmers, but we will not need the millions of programmers that we will be producing if we persist with the current emphasis on programming in computer literacy curricula (Levin and Rumberger, 1983).

Instead of making programming the pinnacle of computer education curricula, we must provide students with "multiple entry points to expertise" (Levin and Souviney, 1983). Multiple entry points will enable students to use computers as powerful tools for a wide range of applications. Some students will develop computer power by learning how to program the machine. Others, however, will gain that power by learning how to use the computer for writing and editing text; for creating music, graphics, and animation; and for organizing and communicating information. Furthermore, one avenue of access does not preclude another. The student who begins learning about computers through programming is not precluded from assembling spread sheets later on. So, too, the student who learns text editing first is not later precluded from learning to program.

Our Approach to Finding Solutions

Our overall goal is to counter the three main problems in current computer use in education:

1. the underutilization of the computer's capabilities
2. stratified access
3. the emphasis on programming as the single avenue to the world of computing

In the next two chapters, we describe the approach we are taking to meet that goal. In Chapter 2, we present some design features of learning environments that can be assembled with computers. These include (1) participation in the whole task and (2) providing dynamic support.

Chapter 3 contains a description of how to use computers as an aid in the writing process, along with a discussion of how a unique collaboration between school teachers and university researchers produced the language arts activities found in Chapters 4-8.

Exploiting The Interactive Capabilities of Microcomputers

The issue of microcomputer use in schools is not one of simply how they can be used in the classroom, but how they can be used to achieve important educational goals that could not be readily achieved without them. It is clear that when computer use is limited to drill and practice and to programming, the full range and power of these machines are not being fully exploited.

Functional Learning Environments

How can computers be used to achieve important educational goals? One way is to exploit the interactive capabilities of microcomputers for language arts instruction. The computer makes it possible to create learning environments which go beyond drill and practice.

In this chapter we explore ways to organize functional learning environments. The functional learning environments we describe adopt a holistic approach to educational practice and provide dynamic support to novices learning to write.

The Whole Task. A fundamental component of our approach to computer use is the belief that chil-

dren learn most effectively by participating in *whole* activities with others. Through this participation in the whole task, others perform some aspects of the task which are too difficult for the children to accomplish on their own. In time, the children learn how to master the entire task alone (Luria, 1976; Vygotsky, 1978; Wertsch, 1979; Flavell, 1981; Griffin and Cole, 1984; and compare Piaget, 1971).

The *holistic* emphasis in our work contrasts sharply with *atomistic* educational process. Children most typically work alone on subparts of a task in school. When they accomplish all the subparts, they are expected to assemble these components into a unified whole on their own. In many standard reading programs, for example, children begin work on recognizing letters, establishing sound-letter correspondence, and blending letters together to read words and sentences. These activities often occur in isolation from discovering reading as a process for learning new things from text. Similarly, when students are asked to write compositions, they typically are asked to start by writing sentences, then paragraphs, and finally complete essays.

A clear example of the holistic approach to educational practice is the way parents teach their young children to read (Ninio and Bruner, 1978). From the beginning, the setting is parent and child,

By Hugh Mehan and Margaret M. Riel

and the activity is reading a book. Initially, the child knows very little about the activity of reading, and the parent must do much of the work. As the child becomes familiar with the patterns, he or she may begin to participate in simple subskills such as turning the pages or pointing to objects. As the child gains knowledge, the parent asks him or her to tell what is happening in the story or to provide names for objects. Slowly, as attention shifts from pictures to words, the child begins to recite well-learned pieces of the story. This skill becomes more and more flexible as the support provided in the book and by the parent recedes, and the child becomes an independent reader.

The *activity*—parent and child sitting together reading the book—has remained constant through the whole process. What has changed is the degree of the child's participation in the activity. This changing network of support has been referred to as "The Zone of Proximal Development" (Vygotsky, 1978; Brown and French, 1979; Griffin and Cole, 1984). The activity that parent and child accomplish ("the zone") provides a good prediction of what the child will soon be able to accomplish on his or her own. This learning to do the pieces in the context of the whole prevents the child from becoming so obsessed with accomplishing subgoals that he or she never understands the relationship of subparts to whole.

Computer literacy involves the mastery of a wide range of machine operations (Bitter, 1982): turning the machine on and off, inserting disks, booting programs, naming machine parts, and manipulating files. In many computer literacy courses, students learn these machine operations separately from actually using the computer. That is, they first name machine parts, then operate the keyboard, printer, and monitor. Once they know the subparts of machine operation, they are introduced to computer applications such as text editing, spread-sheet analysis, or data-base management.

A parallel exists between the relationship that computer literacy has with computer uses and the relationship that reading readiness has with reading in instructional programs such as DISTAR (Becker, 1978). In such programs, reading readiness involves teaching the subparts of the reading process (sound-letter correspondence, word order, decoding operations) prior to and independent of the activity of reading itself. When students master all the components of reading readiness, they are expected to assemble the parts of the reading task into the whole by themselves.

The holistic approach to teaching computer operations to students is analogous to the approach parents take in teaching their children to read. It embeds the teaching and learning of machine operations within reading and writing activities. Instead of being taught machine operations first and computer uses second, students are taught keyboarding, disk management, file maintenance, and editing in the context of learning to write letters, generate school newspapers, and compose poetry. Their language arts lessons—such as correcting the spelling and grammatical errors in a teacher's letter—require that the students operate the computer as well as read and write.

This holistic approach to teaching computer literacy has cognitive and social effects. Initially, students are slow to learn both machine operations and writing skills simultaneously. Their writing production using the computer is lower than it is using paper and pencil. Over time, however, student productivity with the computer improves, and the increase is accompanied by an overall improvement in the coherence of their text and reduction in grammatical and format errors. On a computer literacy test, ninety percent of students receiving the holistic approach—although not given explicit instruction on the mechanics of machine operations—have shown a mastery of basic machine operations (Mehan et al., 1985).

Summary. We have drawn a parallel between a holistic approach to teaching reading (LCHC, 1982) and a holisitc approach to learning to use a microcomputer. In doing so, we asserted that microcomputers can be used to provide children with support for elements of writing tasks they have not yet mastered. Furthermore, this support can gradually be removed as the children become more skillful.

Dynamic Support

Dynamic support refers to the process of systematically decreasing amounts of assistance provided to novices as they progress in expertise and gradually assume parts of the task initially accomplished by an expert. In a properly arranged teacher-student-computer environment, it is possible to create the kind of dynamic support necessary to improve students' writing dramatically.

Riel's research on language disabilities (Riel, 1982) shows how the microcomputer can provide dynamic support. She found that children with language handicaps had greater difficulty in making efficient problem-solving decisions when playing computer games than did a group of students with normal language development. In a follow-up training study, Riel modified the computer software so that, at first, most of the game parameters were controlled by the computer. This support was gradually withdrawn as the players' skill increased. After several weeks, the game performance of both groups was quite similar. The computer had been used to construct a "Zone of Proximal Development," providing training in a variety of systematic, self-regulatory, problem-solving skills as children learned basic materials.

Software is now available which, like the parent teaching reading with the holistic approach, systematically increases the degree and form of learner participation as skills develop. For example, in text editing systems—such as the *Interactive Writing Tools* (Levin, 1982)—texts are constructed which share the initiative between writers and readers along a continuum of support (Riel, Levin, and Miller-Souviney, 1984). This continuum of support is shown in Figure 2.1.

Figure 2.1
A Continuum of Educational Software
(from Riel et al., 1984)

Program Control	Mixed Control	User Control
Static Frames with Fixed Content	Lesson Frames with Content Added	Open Frames with Variable Content

At the program-control end of the continuum, readers of structured interactive text can make simple choices about the direction in a story's plot. At the user-control end of the continuum, an interactive text or planner enables more skilled writers to take complete responsibility for writing. At the user-control end of the continuum, the computer offers high-level suggestions and provides prompts; the machine leaves lower-level writing activities in the hands of the student. By providing activities which range in the degree of support, such writing tools make it easy for students to enter text. Perhaps more importantly, they make it so easy to make changes in text that elementary school students can edit their writing as a functional everyday activity.

Miller-Souviney (1985) used a set of interactive texts to teach expository writing to fourth and fifth graders. Each of the four expository writing tasks was arranged so that students were able to produce a good example of an essay *every* time. In the first activity, "The Sandwich Prompt," the student creates a unique story by choosing among options which are provided throughout the text. Here is the first of several choices that the student makes:

The Sandwich Prompt

Today is
1. Saturday
2. Martin Luther King Jr.'s Birthday
3. Teacher's Workshop Day
4. National Take a Computer to Lunch Day
(Choose 1 . . . 4; 0 to exit);
(Type a number, then push return)

The following portion of a story shows what Michael produced using this program (Miller-Souviney, 1985). The underlined text indicates words actually entered by the student.

The Art of Sandwich Construction
by Michael

Today is National Take a Computer to

Lunch Day and I have a day off from school. My parents are playing tennis so I have to make my own lunch. My specialty is that wonder of culinary art, the sandwich! A great French chef, Francois d'Boloney, taught me to make his most secret recipe, The California Kid's Surprise! . . .

The sandwich making activity gives students a good introduction to the power of word processing. This type of activity, though similar to interactive software such as *Storytree* (Scholastic) and *Storymaker* (Bolt, Beranek, and Newman), is different in a significant way. The stories created with *Interactive Writing Tools* (Encyclopaedia Britannica Educational Corp.) can be saved as text files and subsequently edited with *The Writer's Assistant* (EBE Corp.). Stories generated with *Storytree* and *Storymaker* cannot be modified by the user. Because we feel that students must be able to personalize their work and make corrections easily, the advantage of using the *Interactive Tools* software when teaching writing is an important one.

The second activity in expository writing is an interactive tool which requires students to fill in words and phrases as well as make choices among predetermined options:

School Day Schedule Prompt

The name of my school is
?
(Type, then push CTRL-C when done)
It is in the town of
?
(Type, then push CTRL-C when done)
I am in grade
?
and my teacher's name is
?
I have a very busy schedule at school. My class does all sorts of things to make it fun. . . .

This School Day Schedule Prompt provides students with the beginnings of sentences and para-

graphs, and it invites them to complete the ideas begun by the expository prompter. In the following excerpt from Megan's composition, the text that she entered is underlined:

One Day at School
By Megan

The name of my school is Olive. It is in the town of Vista. I am in grade fourth and my teacher's name is Mrs. Souviney. I have a very busy schedule at school. My class does all sorts of things to make it fun to learn.

The first thing I do is look at the blackboard and copy the daily hand tongue twister. My teacher checks my folder carefully, making sure my writing is nice and neat. . . .

As students' writing skills improve, they take over more and more of the writing activity. In the third expository writing task, students are asked to describe how to run a computer. The program provides a topic sentence for each paragraph along with reminders of what each paragraph should contain. Students enter the introduction, body, and conclusion of their essays.

How to Run an Apple Computer Prompt

We are lucky here at Olive School. We have Apple computers. We use them to help us practice our spelling and math, write stories, and lots of other things. An Apple computer is easy to run. Just follow these simple directions.

First, it is important to know the different parts of the computer and what each does.

(Write complete sentences telling the parts of an Apple and what they do.)
?
(Type, then push CTRL-C when done.)

Next, to start the Apple, several switches need to be turned on.

(In complete sentences, describe where each switch is and what it does.)

?

(Type, then push CTRL-C when done.)

Students respond to each prompt by entering their own sentences and paragraphs. The following paragraphs are part of Michelle's version of how to run a computer; Michelle's text is underlined:

How To Run An Apple Computer
By Michelle

We are lucky here at Olive School. We have Apple computers. We use them to help us practice our spelling and math, to write stories, and lots of other things. An Apple computer is easy to run. Just follow these simple directions.

First, it is important to know the different parts of the computer and what each does. The monitor shows you what you write and the keyboard has letters to type with. The disk drive is where you put the disk in, and the printer is for printing out stories.

Next, to start the Apple, several switches . . . .

The final interactive tool in the expository writing series asks students to think of a topic to write about and gives a few reminders of the composition structure.

How to Prompt

Think of something you know how to do that you could explain to a friend. For example, you may know how to wash dishes, run a computer, or clean your room.

Remember:

1) The first paragraph is your introduc-

tion and will tell something about the activity.

2) The second paragraph will tell the steps it takes to do it.

3) The last paragraph is your conclusion and can tell about how you feel when you finish the activity or when you will do it again.

In this, the fourth expository writing activity, students are now responsible for producing complete texts on their own. Here is part of a story produced by Luis. Note that *all* the text is underlined since the entire composition was entered by the student.

How to Make Money
By Luis

If you want to make money, you must make it right now. If you want to know why, you can say because you would want to help your family, or something else.

To make money, the easiest way could be gathering cans. Cans can be everywhere, so when you are walking and you see a can, stop and . . . .

Throughout these four activities, the goal is for students to keep the quality of their writing constant. As the degree of participation by the learner increases, the amount of support provided by the computer decreases.

QUILL Planners also provide dynamic support for writing. *Planners*, designed primarily as prewriting activities, can help students organize their thoughts and generate ideas for writing. Students subsequently print the ideas generated when using a *Planner* and use the ideas as a guide when composing. The *Planner*-generated text cannot be included in the final composition, however, unless it is reentered by the student.

Teachers can construct *Planners* to provide varying amounts of support for writing. For example, the *Planner* could supply a list of paragraph topic sentences. The student could then order the topic sentences and complete the paragraphs. Since the topic sentences supplied by the *Planner* cannot be saved on disk, they must be reentered as the student composes the paragraphs using *The Writer's Assistant*.

In sum, writing tools such as the *Interactive Writing Tools* and the *QUILL Planners* further facilitate the writing process by providing different degrees of support to the novice writer.

Word Processors and Improved Writing

Word processing systems have been touted as one possible solution to problems in writing (Lipsom and Fisher, 1983). They facilitate the production of manuscripts by minimizing the mechanical details of writing (such as neat script, spelling) and maximizing student attention to the flow of ideas. Spelling verification programs provide assistance in making correction, and printers facilitate the immediate production of neat, professional-looking copy.

We do not think, however, that the word processor itself is responsible for improved writing. Computers cannot, by themselves, solve the problem of teaching students to read and write. The blank screen can be just as intimidating as the blank page (Levin, Boruta, and Vasconcellos, 1983). Students having access to the most powerful editing systems still must approach the task of writing by themselves.

We have found that the microcomputer works most effectively when computer activities are coordinated with tasks in other parts of the curriculum (Mehan, Miller-Souviney, and Riel, 1984). In other words, the microcomputer is most effective when it is integrated into the curriculum rather than treated as an isolated activity, when it is viewed as a tool to meet educational goals rather than as a teaching machine that dispenses knowledge to students.

Writing plays a major role in the curriculum. Students have time to write in personal journals, compose essays on topics generated by the teacher, and write about what they learn in science and social studies.

While we have found that a microcomputer alone cannot transform unskilled writers into skilled ones, it does present an environment which makes possible a new social organization for writing. It is the creation of functional learning environments, not the computer alone, which positively affects the development of student writing.

A Functional Learning Environment: *The Computer Chronicles*

Functional learning environments in language arts are those in which reading and writing are organized for communicative purposes, rather than just as an exercise for a teacher to evaluate (cf. Newman, 1984). The use of computer pen pals, and a student newswire service known as *The Computer Chronicles* (Levin, Riel, Boruta, and Rowe, 1984) are two of the ways in which we have linked reading and writing with communicative purposes. In both cases, students were connected to a normally unavailable audience but one with which they wanted to share ideas. Writing to communicate and not just writing on a microcomputer subordinates the students' concern for the mechanics of writing to the goal of communicating clearly.

The InterLearn Newswire Network is a writing network that links together students from schools in different locations as reporters in a newswire service. The news network is explicitly modeled on commercial international newswire services. Articles can be stored on disk and sent through the mail or, using a modem, over telephone lines. Whenever possible, students' attention is focused on the parallels between their work and the work of professional newspaper reporters and editors.

The InterLearn Network contains a number of crucial features that make it a functional learning environment. First, the software system it uses is designed in ways similar to the "Expository Writing Prompter" described above. *The Computer Chronicles: News Writing Tool* (EBE Corp.) contains a number of onscreen prompts which give the students dynamic support at all phases of the writing process. Second, students work in teams to generate new articles or to edit those received from other locations. These cooperative working sessions facilitate the division of the newspaper writing task among the students. While one student concentrates on the mechanics of writing, another student focuses on the generation of ideas.

Third, cooperative working sessions create a local audience for writing. Since the students work in pairs at the computer center, the presence of another person during the writing proces helps students generate ideas and provides immediate responses to the written text. Fourth, when students realize that other people will read their work for the information it contains and not just to evaluate its form, they take greater interest in the content of their writing. They actively engage in revising and editing their own writing and the texts of their peers.

Summary. Word processing systems such as *Apple Works*, *The Bank Street Writer*, *QUILL*, and *The Writer's Assistant* contribute to the writing process by simplifying the mechanics of entering, editing, and correcting text. The mechanical details of writing are subordinated to the flow of ideas, con-

tent, form, and style. The availability of a printer facilitates student writing since children find the immediate production of neat, professional-looking copy to be highly rewarding and motivating (Malone, 1981; Miller, 1983; Levin et al., 1983; Lipsom and Fisher, 1983).

We recommend the creation of functional learning environments with microcomputers in which reading and writing are arranged for communicative purposes. *The InterLearn Newswire Network* gives readers a goal for writing: to share their ideas and concerns with students with whom they cannot interact directly. The public nature of writing provides motivation for re-writing and editing, giving students increased knowledge of word processing and control over the composing process.

By arranging learning environments in which computer-based support is gradually removed, teachers allow students to gain control of writing by systematically assuming the components of the task initially accomplished by the computer. Dynamic support provided by the interactive capabilities of the computer subordinates the students' concern for the mechanics of writing to the process of writing, resulting in improved quality and fluency.

Computers and The Writing Process

This is a watershed period for American schools. The actions that educators, parents, and the members of the community take now can have a considerable influence on the future course of education. Computers can become stratifiers or equalizers, expensive electronic worksheets or powerful tools to meet educational goals—the choice depending on the actions taken and policies established now.

The role of innovative teachers in this process cannot be overemphasized. Such teachers are often the most knowledgeable people about computers in the educational system. Their expertise places them in an important position to influence both school policy concerning computers and the instructional purposes for which the computers are used. Teachers who are in close contact with students and technology can significantly influence the way students approach computer use. Teachers are in the best position to create functional learning environments which encourage equal access for all students.

By Margaret M. Riel, Barbara Miller-Souviney, and Randall Souviney

Dynamic Support for Teachers

In Chapter 2, we discussed the relationship between the learner, the expert, and the computer system, pointing out the need for dynamic support in the *learning* process. These same relationships hold when we consider the teacher, the students, and the computer system in the *teaching* process.

Riel, Levin, and Miller-Souviney (1984) have proposed a continuum—ranging from program control to user control—that describes the relationship between teachers and educational software (*see* Figure 3.1).

Figure 3.1
Types of Educational Software

Static Frames with Fixed Content	Lesson Frames with Content Added	Programming Languages Authoring Systems
Program Controlled	Mixed Control	User Controlled

At the program-controlled end of the spectrum lies software designed to be used "as is." With this kind of software, users have little or no opportunity to alter the content or presentation of information. Most Computer Aided Instruction (CAI) software fits into this category. To integrate such software into the curriculum, teachers need to organize lessons around the objectives embedded in the software.

Towards the center of the continuum is software which provides the sequence or other structuring frames and the teacher adds the content. An example of this type of software is the *Square Pairs* (Scholastic) in which the teacher supplies the content of a concentration type game and students attempt to make matches. While the content of the software can easily be integrated with ongoing classroom activities, the format of presentation is fixed. Such programs generally provide ways to do "workbook exercises" on the computer and often do not take full advantage of the interactive capabilities of the computer.

Programming languages (BASIC, Logo, Pascal, etc.) and authoring systems (*Interactive Text Interpreter*—used to create *Interactive Writing Tools, QUILL Planners*, or *PILOT*) are at the user-control end of the continuum. These systems enable teachers to create instructional materials consistent with their teaching objectives. Though flexible, such systems often require a considerable investment of teacher time before they can be employed effectively.

Since teachers are learners, too, they can benefit from the same type of "dynamic support" for integrating computer materials into classroom lessons that students do when learning a particular form of writing (*see* Chapter 2). The *Interactive Text Interpreter* is a special-purpose authoring system for designing language arts materials. This simplified programming language, which teachers can learn easily, enables them to use the interactive capabilities of the computer to extend classroom lessons. On the other hand, because teachers with little prior computing experience often lack the confidence and skill to begin designing their own software, programming is not the best entry point for teachers who want to use computers in their classrooms.

Teachers generally introduce computers into their classrooms using software developed by others. As they become more familiar with software and witness their students' success, they may wish to modify existing software packages. The experience of modifying programs leads directly to the skill needed for writing new programs.

The following two scenarios are based on actual classroom observation and interviews (Mehan and Souviney, 1984):

1. One teacher reflected on her initial review of software. Since she knew so little about computers, she felt it was very important that everything run smoothly without her having to make any modifications. Even though she was aware that she could change the software on her own, she initially had no intention of altering programs or writing new ones. As her students began using the software, she became excited by their interest and skill. She watched a number of students (who were working with another teacher) learn not only to use software but also to begin writing their own programs. They began programming by first modifying an existing program, and then they went on to create their own programs. Student success in using and writing software—and the teacher's own increased skill in using the word processing system—led to changes in her attitude towards programming. By the end of the year, she said that she was no longer "phobic," but rather was excited by her ability to create her own materials.

2. Another teacher also started out with minimal knowledge of computers and no exposure to the software described in this book. She observed that the available software did not adequately support instruction for her young, low-achieving, monolingual and bilingual students. When this teacher selected software to use with her class, she had to consider whether it was available in Spanish for her bilingual students. After observing the success and failure of her students with existing software, this teacher decided to try designing her own software materials. After a brief introduction to a word processing system, she began to write her first prompted interactive tool to help students write "friendly letters." Working closely with the author of the English

version of the interactive text, she wrote a Spanish version of the program on her own. After a cooperative editing and debugging session, she introduced the final version of the program as a regular component of the classroom instruction. Then, after completing these materials, she wrote an interactive tool for book reports in Spanish and English. This teacher remains excited about her ability to create interactive programs in two languages that fit within her classroom lessons.

These teachers began using existing software and then changed the programs for their students by substituting familiar names and places for characters and locations, and by changing the on-screen instructions and examples to make them more appropriate for the skill level of their students. After making these changes, the teachers began to write their own programs using an authoring system. Another teacher noticed how much his students enjoyed writing dialogues and wrote a program to help them extend this skill. Yet another teacher wrote a set of programs to help her students develop skill in expository writing (Miller-Souviney, 1985). Several teachers contributed to the development of *The Computer Chronicles: News Writing Tool* to help students learn to write newspaper articles (Levin, Riel, Rowe, and Boruta, 1984).

As teachers acquired the skill and competence to modify existing programs and write new ones, they began thinking about new ways that they could use the computer to help students acquire important academic skills. Our observations indicate that teachers benefit from the same sequence of dynamic support that works so well with students. A description of dynamic support for teacher use and design of software is shown in Figure 3.2.

Figure 3.2
Dynamic Support for Teacher Use and Design of Software

Using Existing Interactive Tools	Minor Changes to Interactive Tools	Using the Toolmaker to Create New Tools	Creating New Tools
Program Controlled		Mixed Control	User Controlled

Summary. This movement from using previously developed programs to modifying programs to creating new programs is what we mean by dynamic support for teachers. Teachers usually begin using software developed by others. Through modifying these programs, they learn how the system works. They can then create new, personalized software systems. Modifying initial examples of software and gradually understanding the organization of the system provides teachers with the dynamic support they need to create computer materials for use in their classrooms.

The Writing Process and the Microcomputer

Despite their power, computers are not able to replace good teaching. Computers are not very good at judging the quality of writing, nor do they interpret adequately the human emotions evident in an author's work. While no computer is able to identify a good joke, computers can be powerful tools when used to support the writing process.

The writing process consists of six interrelated stages:

1. pre-writing
2. writing
3. response
4. revision
5. evaluation
6. post-writing

In a properly organized environment, computer-supported writing systems can have direct application in all six stages of the writing process (Moffit and Wagner, 1976; Cooper and Odell, 1978; Graves, 1978; and Florio-Ruane and Dunn, 1985).

An easy-to-use word processing system, coupled with interactive software, can help busy teachers reinforce good writing habits. As a tool to aid in the writing process, these programs offer students the freedom to express their ideas and experiences by facilitating the composition, revision, and display of their work. The classroom activities presented in Chapters 4-8 are examples of lessons we have found helpful in making the computer a powerful tool in teaching writing as a process.

Pre-Writing. Pre-writing involves the organization of thoughts prior to the act of composing. Before writing on paper or at the computer, students often need to "brainstorm" ideas about a topic. This brainstorming session identifies appropriate descriptive words and often helps formulate the structure of the writing. Pre-writing can be done in a group session or it can be done by each student before beginning a writing assignment. Some teachers prefer to assemble the entire class at once and list pertinent ideas and thoughts on a large piece of butcher paper. Students can then refer to the idea display while composing their writing. Other teachers have their students use a separate sheet of paper to generate descriptive words and organizing phrases.

A fundamental goal during this stage in the writing process is to motivate the students to write. Teachers can accomplish this by building their students' observation skills, creating an appropriate writing mood, and discussing the audience who will read the final compositions. Many teachers have found that the more time they spend motivating students to write, the better the outcome. The following books and task cards offer an excellent selection of pre-writing activities.

1. *The New Language Arts Idea Book* by Joanne Schaff. Glenview, IL: Scott, Foresman and Company, 1985.
2. *Cornering Creative Writing* by Imogene Forte, Mary Ann Pangle, and Robbie Tupa. Nashville, TN: Incentive Publications, 1974.
3. *The Writing Corner* by Arnold B. Cheyney. Glenview, IL: Scott, Foresman and Company, 1979.
4. *If You're Trying To Teach Kids How To Write, You've Gotta Have This Book!* by Marjorie Frank. Nashville, TN: Incentive Publications, 1979.
5. *A Year of Writing Activities* by Dr. I. David

Welch & Susan E. Elliot. New York: Scholastic Book Services, 1979.
6. *Teaching Writing in K-8 Classrooms: The Time Has Come*, by Iris M. Tiedt. Englewood Cliffs, NJ: Prentice-Hall, Inc., 1983.
7. *Teaching Writing, K through 8* by Jack Hailey. Professional Development and Applied Research Center, Department of Education, University of California, Berkeley, 1978.

Pre-writing is the process of exploring words and ideas. Although word processing systems by themselves are not capable of providing the support needed to generate ideas for writing, they can be utilized in the pre-writing stage as a device to record students' ideas as they brainstorm. Computers make it much easier for students to arrange words in clusters, and gathering words to use in writing is an important component of the pre-writing activity. The goal is to have the students generate as many words (and phrases) about a particular subject as possible. Once a list has been established, students can refer to it when writing the first draft of a composition. Figures 3.3 and 3.4 show two examples of word associations that teachers can use for pre-writing (Tiedt et al., 1983).

Figure 3.3
Column Format—Writing About School
school
desk
teacher
student

Figure 3.4
Cluster Format—Birthday Party

Other important pre-writing techniques include improvising, making structural charts, outlining, and taking notes (Hailey, 1978). Because computers are still novel for most students, entering ideas on them may also motivate students' creativity. A large monitor will be helpful if you use the computer to record class lists.

A relatively new way in which the computer can support the pre-writing activity is with interactive software programs designed to help students organize their thoughts prior to writing. Rather than having students begin the writing task with a blank screen, the programs draw the student into the writing task by offering suggestions, giving examples, and asking the students to respond to questions. Selection of different options can also lead to guidance on the structure and sequence of the writing.

For example, *The Computer Chronicles: News Writing Tool* program provides students with a number of possible newspaper articles to write. The students can select among the options or create new ones. With each of the options, students are asked to refine their topics further by creating a headline; they are then given help in organizing the structure of their articles. Their responses to questions and other prompts are saved as the first draft of their article.

Examples of commercially available prompted software which can be utilized for pre-writing are:

Interactive Writing Tools (EBE Corp.)
Sentence Clustering (Milliken)
QUILL Planners (D.C. Heath)
Compu-Poem (K-12 Micro-Media)

Both the *QUILL* writing system and *Interactive Writing Tools* provide the teacher with tools for creating pre-writing activities for their students to use on the computer.

The activity section of this book suggests pre-writing activities for both on and off the computer. For examples of pre-writing lessons, *see* activities 5.3, 5.4, 5.6, 6.1, 6.2, 7.1, 7.2, 7.3, 7.4, 8.1, 8.2, 8.4, and 8.5 in Chapters 5-8.

Writing. The second phase of the writing process is the creation of the first draft of a text. This process involves putting ideas "down on paper"—or on the computer screen. It is the first attempt to flesh out the ideas generated in the pre-writing phase. Student work should not be regarded as finished at this stage.

Writing usually takes place as an individual activity off the computer. Students often benefit from clusters of words and phrases created during pre-writing. Once the initial draft is finished, the students give their essays to either the teacher or peers for a *response*, the next stage in the writing process.

When computer writing tools are available, the writing process takes place at the keyboard, and the composition unfolds on the screen. It is during this phase of the writing process that the computer exerts some of its greatest motivating influence. The ease with which text can be added, changed, moved, or deleted encourages students to try new ideas.

The computer also makes cooperative writing much easier. Students frequently work with a partner when composing at the keyboard. Working with a partner promotes cooperative learning and aids students in their writing. The immediate response of a peer during the initial phase of writing can help students realize how much detail is necessary to communicate an idea. Incomplete idea fragments that might go unnoticed by a solitary writer often elicit a comment such as: "What do you mean?" or "That doesn't make sense." Working with a partner also helps when student writers get bogged down in a particular part of their story. They are apt to give up, perhaps crumpling the paper into a ball and throwing it into the nearest trash can. With the help of a word processor and their peers, students are more likely to move smoothly from pre-writing to writing.

When working with pencil and paper, the phases of writing remain more distinct and sequential than when working with computer writing tools. Pre-writing precedes writing and response. Computer writing tools make it possible for the writer to work at several stages in a more or less parallel fashion. For example, the *Interactive Writing Tools* and *QUILL Planners* can offer onscreen pre-writing activities. Activities included in the *Bank Street Writer Teachers Guide* help students think about topics and organize their thoughts to create a first draft. When students do these activities with peers, the response of the partner to initial ideas can provide valuable guidance in shaping the writing. Since the "first draft" written on a computer is nearly always a component of the final draft, students are more likely to edit throughout the stages of writing when using a word processing system.

Students can sometimes become too concerned with the final product during the writing phase. One of the advantages of using *Planners* or *Interactive Tools* is that they move the students through the production of text without letting them do much revision. Students are told that they will have the opportunity to make changes later when they are working with the word processor. This type of writing software is designed to encourage writing fluency.

Activities 4.5, 4.6, 4.8, 6.3, and 8.6 in Chapters 4, 6, and 8 suggest ways that computer software can be used to help students with the initial composing process.

Response.   The next phase in the writing process involves eliciting a review of one's writing by others. In traditional classroom arrangements, students write alone and the teacher reacts to the students' writing. This procedure reduces the author's audience and range of possible reactions. Teachers can consider including students in the response phase, thereby enabling students to cooperate in the production of a single text. This automatically provides ongoing response during the writing process. In order to encourage peer review, it is often useful to group students in pairs or small groups for the sole purpose of reading and commenting on each other's work. Grouping gives students more responsibility (and frequently motivation for future writing), but it also frees the teacher from reading every word the students write.

Another way to encourage students to respond to each other's work is to make an overhead slide of a student's first-draft story (remove the author's name). The entire class can work as a group to give advice on how to improve the story. Because they know that their stories may be the subject of peer review the next time, students are motivated to offer suggestions.

Another technique for peer review is to have a "read around." After each student's paper is numbered and the author's name removed, it is read to the whole class. Each student assigns points (1-10) to each paper. After rotation around the room, the points are added up and both "good" and "poor" papers are put on overhead slides for discussion.

A printer greatly facilitates the process of peer review. When a student or pair completes an assignment, the text can be printed without a name for anonymous reviews. With printed copies, students cannot easily identify the author or be influenced by the appearance of the handwriting. Consequently, reviewers are forced to deal with the content.

With small groups doing the review process, students can print enough copies for the others in their group. Peers can write comments in pencil on the printouts which are then returned to the writer to help with revision. Authors are able to use the printed copy of their work to make notes for editing later.

The response phase includes comments on the ideas presented as well as on grammar, punctuation, and spelling. It may be preferable to have students focus on only one or two aspects of the review process at a time during response sessions. To cover all aspects, response groups might need to meet several times before the writer makes final changes. The first time, the group might focus on how the ideas are presented and organized, saving for a second time their assessments of the language mechanics such as grammar, punctuation, spelling, and capitalization. Examples of response activities include 6.4 and 8.7 in Chapters 6 and 8.

Revision.   Just as expert authors edit their work before publication, so, too, should novice writers. Editing with paper and pencil is often tedious, and students frequently resist doing it. Teachers must give students *reason* and *motivation* to write. If reason and motivation are established early in a writing assignment, revision usually occurs painlessly.

Students need to understand that initial writing is only a starting place. Even expert writers often produce many drafts before they are satisfied with a piece of writing. Teachers can help students understand the need for revision by sharing revised editions of their own personal writing. Seeing that adults also need to revise their writing helps students view revision as a normal component of the writing process. It may also help to show a piece of writing from the previous year's class—especially a paper which began with clustering and moved through the process to the final draft. By comparing the first and final products, students should be able to see quality differences. Inviting a local newspaper reporter to talk with students about the steps that he or she goes through when producing an article offers another way to communicate the importance of revision.

Some teachers find it helpful to emphasize the difference between early drafts and final ones. Early drafts can be written on newsprint with pencils, while special pencils or pens and "good" paper can be used for final copies. Such an emphasis on the distinction between drafts helps students avoid the mistake of viewing first drafts as final products.

The computer can help the revision process in two important ways. First, it aids the teacher in creating functional writing environments in which students care enough about their writing to do the work of revision. Second, it makes the process of revision much less tedious.

Computers coupled with printers make it practical for teachers to create many different types of writing tasks that the students will find meaningful and motivating. Sharing handwritten information is difficult, and poor handwriting often negatively influences the reader. A computer printout of the text makes every draft easy for others to read and can be used to create a number of different end products that will motivate students to revise their texts.

The editing capabilities of word processing systems reduce the frustration of frequent revision. Corrections do not require recopying the entire work. It is possible to insert a sentence or paragraph in the middle of the text without squeezing words in between, and the number of times that students change or erase a word or phrase while they are composing is not reflected in their final text. The screen does not tear or smear, and the spacing of letters remains uniform. In addition, it has been shown that students introduce fewer *new* errors while making corrections with a word processor than they do when revising hand- or typewritten text (Levin, Riel, Rowe, and Boruta, 1984). The final product also looks so professional that students are more likely to share their work at school and at home.

The natural time to revise is after response groups have met and analyzed a student's text. Because there often is not enough computer time for everyone to review a composition on the video monitor, members of the response group should mark their suggested changes on printed drafts. Writers can then use their assigned computer time to make changes in their compositions with the annotated printed copy as a reference. The final draft can be saved on the student's text disk and subsequently printed.

Activities 5.3, 5.5, 6.5, and 8.8 in Chapters 5, 6, and 8 illustrate how revision of already entered text is an effective way to introduce students to a word processing system. In fact, it is the very ease with which they can revise that seems to motivate many students to learn how to write with a computer.

Evaluation.   Most school writing involves students creating and teachers correcting. The approach to the writing process advocated by Cooper and Odell (1978) and others encourages more input from peers and from adults other than the teacher—e.g., classroom aides, parents, principals, and custodians.

The advantage of using the computer in the evaluation phase of the writing process is the capability it has to produce—with the aid of a printer—neat and professional-looking copies. It is useful to display both first and final copies side by side so that the students can see, firsthand, the progress they have made. Not only is growth measured in this way, but it may motivate students to improve their writing in future assignments.

It is also possible, with some software, to have the computer provide a form of evaluation of the students' writing. For example, *Sensible Speller* (Sensible Software) can be used to mark misspelled words as well as to provide information about the number of misspelled words, the total number of words, and number of unique words. *The Writer's Assistant* and the *Interactive Writing Tools* can be used to collect data on how students write. While the student is writing, for example, these programs can automatically collect the number of corrections made or the number of times a particular word has been used for later review by the teacher.

Student evaluation of others' writing constitutes a vital part of *The Computer Chronicles* newspaper project described in Chapter 8 (*see* Activity 8.9). Students serving on editorial boards review and evaluate articles written by their classmates and students from other schools. An editorial board is a small group of students who are responsible for reading and evaluating articles for possible inclusion in the classroom newspaper.

This peer evaluation adds new dimensions to the writing process. The teacher serves as facilitator while the students themselves take on the more active role of evaluating articles for their newspaper. The concept of an editorial board could work well for other kinds of writing as well. Activity 6.6 provides another example of evaluation.

Post-Writing.   Post-writing refers to the activities that involve the display or presentation of writing to others. Writing that is "published" for others to read helps students understand that communication is the goal of the writing process.

Assembling class books, posting final compositions on office bulletin boards, and inviting visitors to the class for a reading are all ways in which the final products of writing can be shared. Some teachers have found it beneficial to "adopt" another class at their school; the adopted class always hears readings of new compositions first. Older students (grades 5 to 8) can create stories or a book for a younger class (kindergarten or grade 1). They can interview the younger students first to get ideas (pre-writing) and then create a motivating story for their adopted friends to read.

Students are often motivated to write if they know that the materials they create will be donated to the school library at the end of the year. They then become local authors for other students to read. No matter how student writing is shared or displayed, the fact that it is displayed in some way is most important to the students who create it.

Microcomputers and printers make sharing writing much easier. The computer prints out a professional final copy which can be displayed—in books as well as on bulletin boards. Moreover, microcomputers linked to networks (via modems) open up new channels of communication. This technology makes it possible for students across town or around the world to read and evaluate the writing of their peers. By having students communicate with others via an informal newswire service such as the one described in Chapter 8, teachers find that a social studies lesson inevitably occurs as the class discusses the ways their counterparts live.

Suggestions for post-writing activities are described in Chapters 5-8. Sending letters (Activities 5.3 and 5.6), making class books and displays (Activities 6.7 and 7.4), and publishing a newspaper (Activity 8.10) are all ways for students to share their writing with a larger audience than school usually affords.

How a Computer Works

This section describes the function of the basic components of a microcomputer. Teachers who are new users of microcomputers may find this overview helpful as they prepare to introduce the activities in Chapters 4-8. It is increasingly important for teachers to become familiar with the potential and limitations of using microcomputers as tools for learning. While programming skills may not be essential, it is important to know how to operate a microcomputer and how to evaluate instructional software written by others.

Computer programs, or software, are detailed lists of instructions which enable the computer to function as a word processor, a data base manager, a game world, or in many other specialized ways. Thousands of programs are available for popular microcomputers. Good software, like good books, requires considerable creativity and skill to produce. As a consequence, teachers must evaluate software as carefully as they would any other instructional materials prior to use.

Microcomputer Components and Functions. All microcomputers have several "hardware" features in common:

1. Input device—keyboard, mouse, touchpad
2. Output device—monitor and/or printer
3. Microprocessor and memory—central processing unit (CPU), random access memory (RAM), and read-only memory (ROM)
4. Data storage device—floppy disk drive or cassette tape recorder

The keyboard is the most common device for entering information into the computer. Like a typewriter, the computer keyboard has keys that are used to enter letters and other characters and, like the TAB key, to control the position or format of the displayed text.

The monitor screen displays instructions, questions, and graphics to assist in the operation of the software. In word processing, the monitor also displays the text entered on the keyboard.

The printer, another output device, provides a permanent copy of the text when the writing is finished. The more expensive printers are quieter, sometimes faster, and produce better quality type. Most inexpensive printers create the characters by arranging tiny dots (dot-matrix). While not as pleasing to the eye as solid type, dot-matrix printing is quite adequate for most educational applications. Moreover, a dot-matrix printer can provide computer-generated graphics, giving it an advantage over the letter-quality printer in this respect.

Both the word processing program and the text being written are generally stored in temporary memory called RAM (Random Access Memory). Most word processors require that the computer have a minimum of 64 kilobites (64K)—that is,

64,000 characters of memory. When a word processing program is loaded into the computer from either a disk or a tape, a copy of the program is stored in RAM so that the computer will be able to access it quickly. With large programs, the computer may load only part of the program at a time to save room for the text.

Any information typed into the computer must also be stored in RAM. Therefore, part of RAM is used to store the word processing program, and the remainder is available for storing text entered by the user. As a result, there is a limit to the size of the textfiles that the user can write. Most word processors leave enough space in RAM to accommodate about five to ten double-spaced pages of text in a single textfile. This does not mean, however, that there is a limit on the overall length of the text that can be written. Several textfiles can be selected and printed sequentially.

Information stored in RAM is *temporary*. Once the computer is turned off, any information stored only in RAM is lost. The word processing program remains on the disk, but any text entered through the keyboard (input device) and not stored on a disk, tape, or printer (data storage devices) will NOT be saved when the computer is turned off.

All word processing programs have procedures for storing text. Usually, text is stored on a permanent data storage device such as a floppy disk or cassette tape. Generally, it is a different disk or tape from the one used to store the word processing program itself. Using separate text disks provides more space to store text. A convenient form of mass data storage is the floppy disk. When inserted in a disk drive, a magnetic floppy disk can record information. Normally, about 80 double-spaced pages of text can be recorded on one disk, and there is no limit to the number of disks that can be used to store writing. Word processing software generally provides a way for the user to make up new text storage disks from blank disks.

The floppy disk, unlike a cassette tape, permits information to be retrieved in a matter of seconds. Like cassette tapes, however, floppy disks can be damaged by magnets, heat, and fingerprints. The newer hard disk is much more expensive than the floppy disk, but the hard disk can store a vast amount of data.

To enable all these devices to work in unison, every computer has a central processing unit (CPU). The hardworking CPU is a very complex set of circuits which carries out the instructions contained in the software, interprets input from the keyboard, keeps track of information in the memory (RAM), communicates with the user through the monitor screen and printer, and manages the flow of information to and from the disk drive. The CPU can also call on information stored in several read-only memory chips (ROM). Because this type of memory contains information that the computer uses frequently when running many different types of software, it is built into the computer in order to improve efficiency.

As computer technology advances, improved printing, data storage, and input devices will become available. Laser printers, for example, have the potential for generating letter-quality type at current dot-matrix costs. Solid state memory cartridges, which are much faster than disk drives, may replace floppy disks as prices become competitive. Software is already beginning to take advantage of new input devices like the Apple "Mouse" and Koala "Touch Pad." These handy devices facilitate the use of word processors, graphic design software, and other tools. The basic functions of the components remain largely unchanged, however, regardless of the input, output, or storage devices employed.

Getting Started. If you're using an Apple II computer, first place a software disk in the drive and close the door. Turn on both the monitor and the computer. The computer should beep and the disk begin to spin. If the drive buzzes loudly, try opening and closing the drive door. If, after a minute or so, nothing appears on the screen, check to see (1) that the monitor is on, (2) that the power plug is connected to the computer, and (3) that the contrast is set properly. If none of these is the source of the problem, try turning the computer off and then on again.

Good software provides substantial on-screen di-

rections and other help to enable the user to begin quickly. As with any instructional material, however, it is always a good idea to try the software yourself before introducing it to your class. For additional information, consult the documentation supplied with the software and the computer.

Software Evaluation

To help teachers select quality software, several organizations evaluate software products and report the results in an easily accessible form. Many popular magazines specializing in computers and education have sections devoted to software evaluation. The Northwest Regional Education Laboratory supports the Microcomputer Software Information for Teachers (MicroSIFT). MicroSIFT uses teachers to evaluate a wide range of existing software. It then reports their findings in popular computing magazines and the Education Research Information Center (ERIC) data base. Often, a local group of computer-using educators (CUE) can provide the most up-to-date information on available software and may provide access to a software-exchange network.

It is always good practice to preview software before purchasing it. Many software companies offer liberal preview policies for educators. Since high quality software is generally costly, make sure the company is reputable and agrees to replace the product at minimum cost if it proves defective or becomes damaged.

Consider the following characteristics when selecting software for classroom use:

1. **Does the software take advantage of the new technology to present activities that are different from those available with other tools?** Many computer activities can be accomplished more efficiently using another technology. Software that is merely a workbook on disk, for example, may be less efficient than the traditional technology—printed workbooks.

2. **Can the computer activity be integrated with other aspects of the curriculum?** The

computer is a tool to be used by teachers in order to accomplish their educational goals. It is not a teaching machine that operates independently of the rest of classroom activities.

3. **Are the instructions adequate?** All necessary instructions to run the program should be displayed on the screen. One very useful feature in this regard is a continuously displayed instruction window on the screen.

4. **Does the student control the screen advance?** Students vary in the rate at which they can move through activities. As a result, the student—rather than an automatic timer—should control the advance to the next page.

5. **How does the program handle incorrect responses?** Insults, sarcasm, and derogatory remarks are not helpful responses to student errors. The students' character should never be compromised.

6. **Is there an audible response to student errors?** No student should be forced to advertise mistakes to the whole class.

7. **Does the program disproportionately reward failure?** Some programs provide more interesting screen displays when students give incorrect answers than when they give correct ones. No program should make it more fun to fail than to succeed.

8. **How does the program react to errors?** Software should be written so that it will not "crash" if the user accidentally types the wrong key. Incorrect responses should lead to software-initiated help.

9. **Can sound effects be controlled?** While sound can be motivating, it can also be disruptive to other educational activities. The teacher should be able to turn the sound on and off easily.

10. **Does the program contain any factual errors?** The information displayed must be accurate in content, spelling, and grammar.

11. **Does the documentation explain how to use the software, and does it provide suggestions for classroom applications?** Demand the same level of quality in a software program's teachers' guide as you do in the materials accompanying a textbook or other teaching aid.

12. **Does the software publisher provide a reasonable means for acquiring a backup copy of the program and replacement of damaged disks?** Software publishers should recognize the unique vulnerability of magnetic disks and offer low-cost replacements.

Summary

This chapter, in which we have described the use of the computer as a tool to support the writing process, serves as a transition between the general framework of Chapters 1 and 2 and the specific language arts classroom activities presented in Chapters 4-8.

Teachers as well as students can benefit from a system of dynamic support. Teachers can begin by using software developed by others and getting advice from more experienced educators in their area. As teachers become more familiar with the limits and possibilities of computer uses, they may begin to modify existing software or, in some cases, to design their own. Gradually, the need for outside support will diminish as teachers gain confidence in selecting and using language arts (and other) software in the classroom.

Since the language arts activities that are presented in Chapters 4-8 are the product of dynamic support, they cannot be expected to stand on their own. They are intended to be provocative guidelines for the innovative teacher, not definitive instructional packages that must be implemented precisely as written. It is our hope that teachers will continue to experiment with creative ways to use computers in their instruction in order to provide equal access to computer technology for all children.

Introducing The Classroom Computer

Overview of Classroom Activities

Chapters 4-8 contain sets of activities designed to introduce the use of a word processor for writing in grades 4-8. These activities assume only minimal computing experience on the part of the students or teacher. Some of the writing activities do *not* require a computer and others do. Even with access to only one classroom computer, these activities can be completed by all the students in a class over the period of a school year. Depending on student interest, many of the activities may be repeated.

The activities in this chapter offer several ideas for introducing the word processor for student writing. The remaining activity sequences take the writer through the six steps of the writing process as described in Chapter 3. "Writing Letters" (Chapter 5), "Writing Poetry" (Chapter 6), and "Expository Writing" (Chapter 7) offer structured writing experiences for these specific types of writing. The final set of activities in Chapter 8 provides a guide for the development of a classroom or school newspaper using articles written by students—and perhaps those from other classrooms or schools.

In order to make the activity instructions as specific as possible, we have employed the Apple IIe computer and selected software as examples. Other machines and appropriate software can be substituted as required.

Classroom Organization

While computers can be used to help teach the writing process in a lab setting, this book offers guidance to the teacher who is using the computer in the classroom. The assumption is that the teacher has one computer with one disk drive and access to a printer. The availability of but one computer for 30 or more students presents teachers with the problem of facilitating equal access. Providing equal access to all students depends on a systematic management system which effectively utilizes the computer time available. Since an important principle of any computer management system is independence, students need to be encouraged to become independent computer users who do not constantly seek help from the teacher.

Because computer technology is likely to influ-

By Kim Whooley, Randall Souviney, and Bea Liner

ence everyone's lives in the future, it is important for teachers to insure that boys and girls of all achievement levels and socioeconomic backgrounds be included in computer activities. Careful scheduling is vital in order to accomplish this goal. In order to use a computer in the classroom effectively, teachers must determine appropriate educational goals for students, plan the curriculum, and identify areas where the computer can be used to help accomplish these goals.

Several organizational decisions must be made about ways to make the computer a part of the classroom learning environment. Some of these organizational decisions concern the use of time and space in the classroom. Teachers must decide how many students will work at the computer at one time, and they must determine the length of work periods, the content of the instruction, and how the computer activities coordinate with learning experiences throughout the school day.

Computers fit easily into classrooms which are organized to include learning centers. A "computer center" becomes a natural complement to this type of classroom arrangement. It is just as important to establish the educational goals for a computer center as it is for any other learning center or activity. Similarly, the planning and work that goes into the design of any activity center is the same planning and work that goes into the design of a computer center. Once the teacher determines activities for

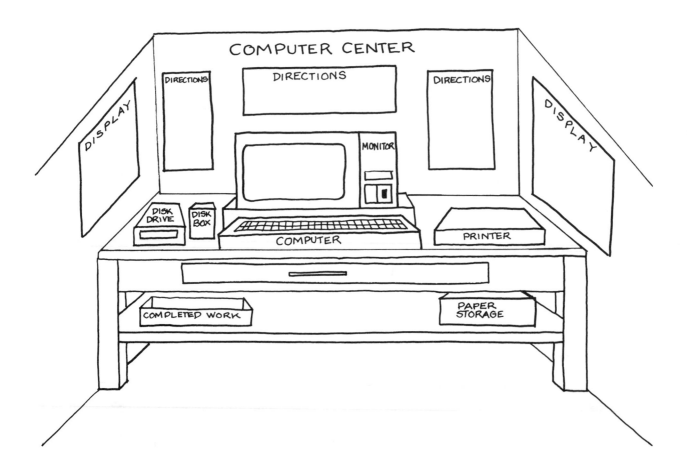

each center, students must be allocated to work groups, time at each center must be rationed, and the coordination of activities between centers must be arranged. Detailed activities for setting up a computer center in a classroom are described later in this chapter.

The activities in this book were written by teachers who found it effective for students to work in pairs at a computer center. Each pair of students can be scheduled for 25- to 30-minute periods through the school day, which means that each student should receive two sessions per week at the computer. Recent studies of computer-supported writing indicate that two students collaborating at the keyboard obtain cognitive and social benefits which do not accrue to students working alone (Mehan et al., 1985; Trowbridge and Durnin, 1984). It has also been found that paired workers interrupt the classroom less frequently than do students working alone.

Introducing the Computer.   Teachers working with a computer for the first time often find it helpful to start by organizing a whole class demonstration of computer operations and the basic word processing features. They begin by introducing students to the computer keyboard. Although the layout of the computer keyboard is similar to that of a typewriter, there are some important differences. For example, a number of "control keys" elicit special features of the computer's operations. A number of commercial programs promote familiarity with the keyboard. These include *Kids on Keys* (Spinnaker), *Typing Tutor* (Simon and Schuster), *Master Type* (Scarborough Systems) and *Apple Presents Apple* (Apple Corporation). These programs help students develop familiarity with the keyboard without separating the development of computer operation skills from the larger task of learning to write with a computer.

Wall displays are also helpful in promoting computer familiarity. For example, teachers can make a giant keyboard display by writing each letter or symbol on a styrofoam hamburger carton (available at fast-food restaurants) and arranging the cartons on a bulletin board in a configuration matching that of the computer keyboard. Constructed early in the year, this display can become a ready reference for children first learning the character positions. Likewise, conveniently placed written instructions can facilitate students' learning of computer skills. Placing posters and cards with instructions about the care and feeding of the computer, basic text editing commands, and special instructions for each assignment also serve as helpful reminders. Even providing students with access to one or more old typewriters can increase the amount of classroom keyboard experience available to them.

Teachers have found it helpful to set up a "typing center" to accompany the computer center. Activities scheduled for this center might include the typing of spelling lists and vocabulary words, writing letters and messages to other students, and working on structured typing lessons involving home-key placement. It is important to keep in mind that it is not necessary for students to become proficient typists in order to operate the computer's keyboard. Student enjoyment and proficiency are likely to increase, however, with keyboard mastery.

Setting Up a Computer Center.   A computer center allows students maximum access to a limited amount of specialized equipment without removing the students from the classroom. It also gives students an opportunity to gain computer operation skills within the standard curriculum. A learning center arrangement also offers the teacher a range of scheduling options within the classroom.

The following activities set out a plan for implementing a computer center in a standard classroom. The activities assume full-time access to one computer with a single disk drive and a printer. Upon completion of the series of activities in Chapter 4, grade 4-8 students should be able to:

1. Boot and run other software designed for instructional purposes

2. Demonstrate basic familiarity with computer operation, text storage, and disk management

ACTIVITY 4.1 THE PENCIL AS WORD PROCESSOR

Objective. To introduce the teacher and students to the concept of word processing by comparing writing with a pencil to writing with a computer

Time Allotment. 30-minute whole group session

Materials.
—A pencil with an eraser
—Writing With a Pencil Chart (Blackline Master 1 in Appendix)
—Writing With a Word Processor (Blackline Master 2 in Appendix)
—List of word processing features (*see* below)

PROCEDURE

Once you know how to use a computer for writing, it is easy to take the concept of word processing for granted. The novice, however, might find it useful to compare writing with a computer to writing with a more common technology, the pencil.

A good way to introduce a new idea is to compare it to something that is well known. In this case, you can draw an analogy between one of the most widely used forms of technology for writing, the pencil, and the newest form of technology for writing, the computer. Ask your students to imagine that someone who had never seen a pencil had just bought one and that you had to give the person written directions on how to use it. Your directions, or documentation, might look something like the following (*see* Blackline Master 1 in Appendix):

Writing With a Pencil

To Write:
1. Move the PENCIL to the place where you want to write.
2. PUT THE LEAD POINT DOWN.
3. WRITE the words.
4. When finished, LIFT THE PENCIL.

To Erase:
1. Move the PENCIL to the spot you wish to erase.
2. PUT THE ERASER END DOWN.
3. Move the ERASER over the words to be removed.
4. When finished, LIFT THE PENCIL.

Demonstrate each of the pencil steps. Next, introduce the computer word processor as a new technology for writing that in many ways is very similar to using a pencil. The computer also comes with documentation on how to use it.

Here is a similar list of steps for writing and erasing with a word processor. Notice that only the words in capital letters are changed. These instructions are written specifically for *The Writer's Assistant*, but you can easily change the commands on the task card to coordinate with another word processor. If you have a computer with a large monitor, you may wish to demonstrate each operation, but it is often just as effective to operate an imaginary computer.

Writing With a Word Processor

To Write:
1. Move the CURSOR to the place where you want to write.
2. PRESS I FOR IN.
3. TYPE the words.
4. When finished, PRESS CTRL-C.

To Erase:
1. Move the CURSOR to the spot you wish to erase.
2. PRESS D FOR DROP.
3. Move the CURSOR over the words to be removed.
4. When finished, PRESS CTRL-C.

Emphasize the way in which the "documentation" for the two methods of writing are very similar. Since all students know how to write with a pencil, they can use this knowledge to help in learning how to use a computer for writing.

Finally, discuss the differences between the pencil and computer writing technologies. First, the pencil is a two-function writing tool: write and erase. Although the computer is like a pencil, it has many more functions and capabilities. Show a list of categories of word processing functions like the following (for *The Writer's Assistant*):

1. Changing Text—Insert, Drop, eXchange, Replace, Word

2. Moving Through the Text—Page, Jump, Find

3. Moving Text Around—Mix, Align, Transfer, Copy

4. Adjusting the Writing Environment—Set Parameters

Some word processing systems also allow users to see the instructions (documentation) for each command on the screen while they are writing. While it would be difficult to write the directions for using a pencil on the pencil itself, the computer has no problem storing such information. In *The Writer's Assistant*, for example, the Help command tells how to use any of the other features.

ACTIVITY 4.2 DEVELOPING FAMILIARITY WITH THE KEYBOARD

Objective. To familiarize students with the typewriter keyboard and to provide an opportunity for them to practice and increase typing skills before actually using a computer

Time Allotment. 5-minute whole group session 30-minute session per week for each student pair for 2-3 weeks

Materials.
—One or two electric typewriters
—Typing paper
—Typing Center Task Card (Blackline Master 3 in Appendix)
—Typing Center Directions (Blackline Master 4 in Appendix)
—Rotation and Schedule (Blackline Masters 5 and 6 in Appendix)

PROCEDURE

In a whole group session, give a brief overview of the typing center. Demonstrate how to turn the machines (electric typewriters) on and off, how to insert paper, and how to use the shift, tab, and return keys.

Schedule students to work in pairs in the typing center for one 30-minute period once a week for two or three weeks. Set up the typewriters in a convenient area of the classroom. Make sure the necessary materials and task cards which describe the typing activities are readily available. Posters displayed at the center are used to provide instructions on proper use and care of materials.

ACTIVITY 4.3 INTRODUCING THE COMPUTER

Objective. To help students become familiar with basic machine

operation and to learn to run a piece of software

Time Allotment. 45-minute whole group session

Materials.
—Apple II computer
—*Apple Presents Apple, Typing Tutor,* or *Kids on Keys* software
—Disks, storage box, table

PROCEDURE

Arrange the class so that everyone has a good view of the computer. Ask your students the following questions to gauge their current understanding of the microcomputer's basic components.

Sample Questions

a. Can you name the parts of this computer? (keyboard, monitor, disk drive, central processing unit and memory)

b. Who can tell what each part does? (keyboard used to enter information; monitor used to display information; disk drive used to record information on disks; CPU is the computer's "brain" which controls and manipulates information; memory temporarily stores information for the CPU)

c. How do you turn the machine on? (procedure varies from machine to machine)

d. What is a floppy disk used for? (long-term storage of information)

e. Can anyone describe how a computer works? (information entered through the keyboard is processed by the CPU and stored in temporary memory; the results may be displayed on the monitor screen or saved on disk)

Answers to questions like these should help guide additional instruction required to complement students' current knowledge. Students with more computer experience should be able to provide valuable information for their less experienced peers. Try to let the students give information in their own words as much as possible.

After identifying the basic components, have a student follow your directions for inserting the *Apple Presents Apple* disk into the drive and turning on the machine. Use this opportunity to have students role play proper care and treatment of equipment. Have them formulate commonsense rules for usage, generating charts of rules and directions to be used later at the computer center.

Once the *Apple Presents Apple* software has been "booted," it should be self explanatory. Clear instructions for its use should appear on the monitor screen. Have students take turns following the screen-displayed instructions so that as many students as possible have an opportunity to use the computer. Allow students to run through as much of the program as their interest allows. It is not necessary for them to see the entire program since they will have ample time to do so when working in pairs during the next activity.

Be sure to allow adequate time for a review at the end of the demonstration. Have students demonstrate the correct procedures for inserting the disk, turning on the machine, and so forth. By allowing students to ask each other questions concerning these activities, you increase the likelihood that attention will be focused on the least understood areas.

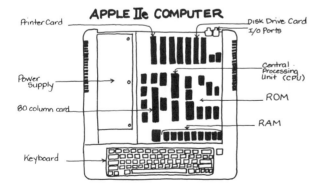

APPLE IIe COMPUTER

Printer Card
Disk Drive Card
I/O Ports
Power Supply
Central Processing Unit (CPU)
80 column card
ROM
RAM
Keyboard

ACTIVITY 4.4 USING THE COMPUTER CENTER

Objective. To learn how to run a piece of software in the computer center

Time Allotment. 5-minute whole group session 30-minute computer session for each student pair

Materials. —Apple II computer
—*Apple Presents Apple, Typing Tutor,* or *Kids on Keys* software
—Computer Help Charts (Blackline Masters 7, 8, and 9 in Appendix)

PROCEDURE

In a 5-minute whole group session, go over the schedule for pairs working at the computer center. The general rules in effect for using a center in the classroom should apply. Emphasis should be placed on following the instruction charts displayed at the center and the directions presented on the computer screen (*see* Blackline Masters 7, 8, and 9 in Appendix).

Establish a consistent procedure for requesting help in times of difficulty. Although the procedure may well vary from classroom to classroom, you might select two or three students to act as "computer tutors." These students should be able to demonstrate a clear understanding of computer operation procedures and be adept at independent problem solving. Consider appointing children who have not met with much success at school in the past to receive the special computer tutor training. This experience will provide such children with a new opportunity to excel in the classroom.

Schedule pairs of students into the center for about 30 minutes each, throughout the day if possible. Everyone should have an opportunity to run *Apple Presents Apple* (or one of the other suggested programs) in a period of one week. Depending on student interest, you may want to extend the activity for an additional week using the same or alternate software.

The microcomputer, monitor, disk drive, and software storage container should be set up in a manner similar to that shown in the Computer Center Diagram. Although placement of the center will depend in part upon the availability of electrical outlets, it should be oriented so that the screen is not easily visible from the rest of the room. Do not place the computer center in close proximity to any major teaching areas, but do position it so that you can see it from most areas of the room. It should be enclosed on three sides (to limit access to the area), and it should have adequate display space for posting written directions.

Center direction charts should be clear and concise. Although operating the software program used for this activity should pose few problems for students, they may need some support in hardware use and commands.

ACTIVITY 4.5 WRITING WITH INTERACTIVE SOFTWARE

Objective. To introduce procedures for using *Interactive Writing Tools* without saving text on disk

Time Allotment. 30-minute whole group session

Materials. —Apple II (64K) computer
—Interactive story writing tool (*Narrative Writing Tool* by EBE Corp., *Story Tree* by Scholastic, or *Storymaker* by Bolt, Beranek, and Newman)

PROCEDURE

Group students so that they are all able to see the monitor. Explain that the computer can be used as a sophisticated kind of a typewriter and that they will learn how to use a computer program to help them write stories, poems, and letters. Ask for a volunteer to insert and boot the story-writing program (e.g., *Narrative Writing Tool*). Having students assist in demonstrations provides an opportunity for reviewing command procedures.

Once the program has been "booted" (entered into the computer's memory), students should be able to follow the directions displayed on the screen to complete the writing task (though they may need to be reminded occasionally). When the story is finished, the *Narrative Writing Tool* program asks the student to name the text in order to save it on a disk. For this activity, however, students will *not* save their text (*see* Activity 4.7 for saving text).

The following sequence is for *Interactive Writing Tools* (InterLearn and EBE Corp.). Other programs do not allow the students to save their work.

You will see:
Do you want to see the text you just created on the screen?
Press Y (for Yes) and the story will be shown on the screen.
Do you want to save your text?
Type N (for No) and you will see:
Are you sure you want to LOSE your text?
Type Y (for Yes).
If a printer is attached to your computer system, you will see:
Do you want to print that text?
Press Y (for Yes) and a copy of the story will be printed.

Encourage students to run the program with as little teacher assistance as possible. It is important to establish the practice of relying on screen directions and one's partner for help. If you use computer tutors, remind the students to call upon the tutors—not you—in times of trouble. *Interactive Writing Tools* are self explanatory and work well for this activity. Students enjoy making the prompted choices and entering their own text as they work through the activity.

ACTIVITY 4.6 INDEPENDENT USE OF INTERACTIVE SOFTWARE

Objective. To create stories independently using *Interactive Writing Tools*

Time Allotment. 30-minute computer session for each student pair

Materials. —Apple II (64K) computer
—*Interactive Writing Tools* (InterLearn and EBE Corp.) or *Storymaker* (BBN)

PROCEDURE

Following the computer center schedule, the posted directions, and the screen-displayed instructions, students work in pairs to generate stories. Students should be encouraged to create as many stories as their time allows. Students should *not* save this first set of stories on disk. The compositions should be displayed on the monitor and printed. You may want to have the students print two copies of their stories, one for the teacher and one to take home.

ACTIVITY 4.7 SAVING YOUR WORK— INTRODUCTION

Objective. To learn the procedures for storing student stories on disk for later editing

Time Allotment. 30-minute whole group session

Materials.
—Apple II (64K) computer
—*Interactive Writing Tools* software
—Text storage disk (WA-TEXT: *Writer's Assistant* Text Disk)
—Naming It Chart (Blackline Master 10 in Appendix)
—Naming Codes Chart (Blackline Master 11 in Appendix)
—Saving It Chart (Blackline Master 12 in Appendix)
—Finding It Chart (Blackline Master 13 in Appendix)

PROCEDURE

Seat students so that they can all view the monitor screen. Boot an *Interactive Tools* disk and allow students to make text selections as you enter their choices. When you have completed a story, discuss with students the disadvantage of losing the text when they quit the program. Explain that there is a way to save the story in a "computer notebook" so that they can look at it again later. Display the step-by-step instruction charts for naming and saving text on disk (Blackline Masters 10, 11, 12, and 13 in Appendix).

Although several methods exist for naming files in a way that makes it easy for students to identify stories at a later date, the class should agree upon one system in order to minimize disk management

---

NAMING CODES

1	Karen	L	Chelsea
2	Tim	M	Linda
3	Michelle	N	Rahn
4	Bud	O	Cheri
5	Margaret	P	Will
6	Randy	Q	Norma
7	Barbara	R	Isabel
8	Bea	S	Kathy
9	Luis	T	
A	Bobbie	U	
B	Marty	V	
C	Christie	W	
D	Cyndy	X	
E	Gloria	Y	
F	Steve	Z	
G	Marcia		
H	Jim		
I	Michael		
J	Megan		
K	Kim		

Kind of Writing

MP - Monster Poem
SS - Silly Sentences
AA - Animal Antics
SW - Star Wars
CP - Computer Pals
EW - Expository Writing

---

problems as students create more and more text to be stored and retrieved.

Encourage students to read and follow the direction sequence for saving, displaying, and printing text after completing their compositions. Allow students who make mistakes to use the opportunity for troubleshooting. When you have successfully demonstrated the series of directions for storing text on the text disk, review the procedure several times by having individual students demonstrate the complete sequence.

ACTIVITY 4.8 SAVING YOUR WORK— PRACTICE

Objective. To learn how to store text created with _Interactive Writing Tools_ on disk for later editing and printing

Time Allotment. 30-minute computer session per student pair for one or two weeks

Materials. —Apple II (64K) computer
—_Interactive Writing Tools_ or other prompted writing programs
—Text storage disk (WA-TEXT: _Writer's Assistant_ Text Disk)
—Direction Charts (Blackline Masters 10, 11, 12, and 13 in Appendix)

PROCEDURE

Schedule pairs of students to work at the computer center. Using wall charts showing necessary computer commands and screen-displayed directions, have the students use the same _Interactive Writing Tool_ as in the previous activity. When the students have completed the task, have them name and save their text.

You may want to extend this activity into a second week, depending on how quickly your students learn to manage the commands for saving text on the text disk. And you may find it helpful to appoint a computer tutor at this time because their first use of the two different disks (software disk and text disk) may confuse some students.

Once they have saved the stories they create with the prompted writing environments (_Interactive Writing Tools_), students are ready to learn how to use a word processor to make changes in their work. Chapter 5 presents a series of activities to introduce this aspect of word processing to your class.

Writing Letters: Learning The Editor Commands

The activities in Chapter 5 are intended to teach students to use a word processor. Word processors generally contain a dozen or more editing commands to allow the user to make changes in the content or format of a composition. Beginning students, however, need to learn only a few commands to get started writing. Once they have learned the basic commands to Insert, Drop, and Save text, they should be ready to begin writing letters. As they gain experience, additional commands may be introduced.

Teachers have found it efficient for students to practice editing text or compositions that have been previously entered with prompted writing environments like *Interactive Writing Tools* (EBE Corp.). Students can use text created by a program like *The Letter Writer* (EBE Corp.), the *QUILL Mailbag* (D.C. Heath), or a letter previously entered by the teacher. Letters that contain errors give students practice in using a word processor to make repairs. As students become skilled, they should be able to compose text directly on a word processor.

Without careful management, students and teachers may lose track of text files, or they may

By Barbara Miller-Souviney and Randall Souviney

create a text file having the same name as another student. Two files on one disk cannot have the same name. To avoid such problems, students should be divided into groups and assigned to a text disk labeled with a number or colored sticker. Usually, four to six elementary students can be assigned to a disk without filling it too quickly. Older students, however, may require their own disks. Posting a list of students using each disk makes it easier for students to find the correct disk when writing or editing previous drafts. When a disk becomes filled, old files can be printed and removed, or a new disk can be created.

As students begin to generate larger amounts of text, it is important to organize student work systematically on disks. When students enter and store a piece of writing (text), a disk file is created and stored on the text disk. The length of a file name is limited (e.g., 10 characters for *The Writer's Assistant*). You may wish to use a special code (like the student's initials) for naming files in order to help keep track of the large number of files created during a few weeks of writing (*see* Blackline Master 10 in Appendix). The following three methods for organizing student files on disk have been successful:

1. *Topic Disk.* For this simple method of

management, label a disk with the name of the current writing topic (e.g., haiku poetry, newspaper articles, letters). All students in the class use this disk to store appropriate files, naming each file with their initials or first names. As you introduce new topics to the class, label new disks and keep them near the computer. You can prepare other topic disks and keep for future activities. This method works best for beginning writers.

2. *Group Disk.* Another method of organizing student files is to color code disks according to existing student groupings (e.g., reading groups). Each group of four to six students always store their text on the same disk which they recognize by its colored dot. In this arrangement, each file name should include information about the writer and the activity topic. As new topics are introduced, old files can be removed or moved to a storage disk, or a new disk can be created.

3. *Individual Disk.* As students gain facility using the word processor and begin to write longer files, it may be more convenient to issue each student (or pair of students) a personal text disk. In this arrangement, only information about the topic and perhaps the date need to be included in the file name. All personal writing can be stored on this disk. New text disks can be added or old files removed as necessary.

General Overview

The following activities will help students understand and use a text editor (*The Writer's Assistant, QUILL,* or other word processing system) to write letters. By using simple editing commands (In, Drop, Quit, Update), students will learn to write letters which can be exchanged with "computer pals" in other classrooms. By using the computer to create

new audiences, students will see the communicative value of using the computer as a tool for writing.

Although any text editor can be used with the following activities, the examples use *The Writer's Assistant* (EBE Corp.) which is also used in *QUILL* (D.C. Heath). It is not necessary to know all the features of a text editor system before introducing it to young children. The following editing commands, along with cursor movement commands, will allow students the opportunity to engage in many different writing activities for a year.

Editor Commands for The Writer's Assistant

I = In for typing in text
D = Drop for removing text
H = Help for learning commands
Q = Quit for saving text
CTRL-C = CONTROL-C (to keep or "lock in" text)

Cursor Movement—LEFT and RIGHT ARROWS, TAB (Apple IIc and IIe), RETURN, SPACE, UP and DOWN ARROWS (Apple IIc and IIe), or O = up, L = down (Apple II and II+)

As students gain editing experience, more sophisticated commands can be introduced. Teachers should review *The Writer's Assistant User's Guide* or the *QUILL* teacher's guide to make sure they are familiar with the function of each command. As in all writing activities (with or without the computer), large group demonstrations are well advised prior to individual work. To help students stay on task and become independent, post large charts listing the editing commands and other directions near the computer.

If any of the *Interactive Writing Tools* (EBE Corp.) are used to compose and save text on a text disk, the results may be edited directly utilizing *The Writer's Assistant.*

After completing the activities in Chapter 5, students should be able to:

1. Operate a microcomputer with sufficient skill to compose and edit an original text using a word processor

2. Write friendly and business letters utilizing the correct format

ACTIVITY 5.1 MOVING THE CURSOR

Objective. To learn how to move the cursor around the screen

Time Allotment. 30-minute whole group computer session

Materials. —Apple II (64K) computer
—*Writer's Assistant* system disk (WA-SYS:), *QUILL* system disk, or other word processor
—Text disk to store students' work (WA-TEXT:)
—Cursor Movement Chart (Blackline Master 14 in Appendix)

—Paragraph stored on WA-TEXT: Disk
—Cursor Movement Task Card (Blackline Master 15 in Appendix)

PROCEDURE

Prior to the lesson, enter the following paragraph and save it on the text disks for the students to work with:

This paragraph was entered by your friendly teacher. You see, I, too, am learning to use the computer as a tool for writing. Together, I hope we will learn to write using a computer. We will be doing all kinds of writing on the computer. We will write letters, poetry, stories, and even a classroom newspaper. If we work hard, we can all become better writers.

In a large group setting, display the Cursor Movement Chart (*see* Blackline Master 14 in Appendix) and review "Cursor Movement Keys" with the group. Invite students to come up to the computer and move the cursor to different places in the text (e.g., put the cursor over the first letter in the word "friendly," then move the cursor over the last letter in the word "newspaper"). Repeat the process until the students understand how to move the cursor up, down, left, and right. Be sure to explore the use of the RETURN and SPACEBAR keys. Other cursor movement activities include:

1. Make a maze on an overhead transparency and tape the transparency over the monitor screen. Have the students move the cursor through the maze using the cursor movement keys.

2. Make task cards (*see* Blackline Master 15 in Appendix) which give directions for students to find "secret" letters, words, and punctuation marks coordinating with a previously stored paragraph.

3. Have pairs of students time each other as one student points to a spot in the text and the other tries to move the cursor quickly to that spot.

ACTIVITY 5.2 INTRODUCING THE WORD PROCESSOR

Objective. To learn to enter, save, and print a short paragraph

Time Allotment. 30-minute whole group computer session
30-minute computer session working in pairs

Materials. —Apple II (64K) computer
—*Writer's Assistant* system disk (WA-SYS:)
—Text disk to store students' work (WA-TEXT:)
—Sample paragraph written on a chart
—Editing Command Chart (Blackline Master 16 in Appendix)
—Opening screenfulls for *The Writer's Assistant* (Blackline Master 17 in Appendix)

PROCEDURE

Write the paragraph below—or one of your own creation—on a chart. In a whole group setting, tell students that they will be typing (entering) the paragraph into the computer. Read the paragraph together.

Learning to write on a computer is easy. Just think, no more worn out erasers, no more torn paper, and no more writing everything over again. A word processor makes it simple to correct writing mistakes. If you have a printer, you can print your work by pressing a key. It may even make writing more fun.

Using the WA-SYS: Disk and the WA-TEXT: Disk, each pair of students should enter this paragraph into the computer during their scheduled computer time. Point out the labels on each disk so that the class will be able to tell them apart. The *systems* disk (WA-SYS:) contains the word processor program. The *text* disk (WA-TEXT:) is used to store student writing. Putting different colored labels on each will help the class keep them separate.

Explain that the WA-SYS: Disk needs to be "booted"—put into the drive and the Apple turned on—first. If you have a single disk drive system, on-screen prompts will help the user insert the WA-TEXT: Disk at the appropriate time. If you have two disk drives, put WA-SYS: in drive 1 (called drive 4 in Pascal) and WA-TEXT: in drive 2 (called drive 5 in Pascal).

Have a volunteer come to the front of the class to boot the WA-SYS: Disk. The opening screen for *The Writer's Assistant* presents the following four choices (*see* Blackline Master 17 in Appendix):

1. The Writer's Assistant
   For writing and revising texts
2. The Printing Press
   For printing the text files
3. The File Cabinet
   For organizing files on your disk
4. The Initializer
   For preparing brand-new disks

Select the first option on the menu by pressing the numeral 1. For a single drive Apple system, the screen will prompt the user to remove the WA-SYS: Disk, insert the WA-TEXT: Disk, and then press L. The user will be asked to enter his/her name (initials or first name up to 10 characters). The user is then asked:

What text do you want
to work on?

Explain that each student pair will need to create a new text file by naming the text they are about to enter. First names or initials work well as text file names. Have the volunteer enter his/her initials and press RETURN. The computer will look to see if this name has been used before. If it has, the volunteer must choose a new one. If it hasn't, the screen will show:

[INITIALS].TEXT is new. Is that OK?

The user should press Y (for Yes). It is not necessary to press RETURN. The disk will spin and a command line will be presented across the top of the screen:

> In / Drop / Quit / Help / ?

Show the Editing Command Chart, and explain that In, Drop, Quit, and Help are the commands that can be used for writing. To enter text, have the volunteer press I (for In) and then start typing the paragraph. Explain that the whole paragraph can now be entered. A mistake can be erased by using the back-arrow. The computer even moves to a new line when it runs out of room. (*Note*: If you have an 80-column board, you can type about 80 characters on a line. Older Apples may allow only 40 characters per line. See the *User's Guide* for instructions on Setting the Environment to adjust line length.)

When the paragraph is entered, press CTRL-C to "lock in" the text. Finally, press Q (for Quit) and U (for Update) to save the text on the WA-TEXT: Disk. At this point, if a printer is attached to the computer, the user will be asked:

Print out this text?

Press Y (for Yes) for a quick printout of the paragraph.

ACTIVITY 5.3 FRIENDLY LETTERS

Objective. To learn the format of a friendly letter and use In and Drop editing commands

Time Allotment. 30-minute whole group computer session
30-minute computer session working in pairs

Materials.
—Apple II (64K) computer
—*Writer's Assistant* system disk (WA-SYS:)
—Text disk to store student's work (WA-TEXT:)
—Editing Command Chart (Blackline Master 16 in Appendix)
—Editing Letter Chart (Blackline Master 18 in Appendix)
—Friendly Letter Task Card (Blackline Master 19 in Appendix)
—Previously entered friendly letter

PROCEDURE
Enter the following friendly letter before the lesson Name the text file FRIENDLY.

May 15, 1986

Dear Computer Pal,

My name is Russell and I am a cat. I have long orange and white fur. My paws and belly are white. I weigh 17 pounds in the winter and 14 pounds in the summer. I shed my fur (and some fat). I was born in a foreign country named Papua New Guinea.

My owner tries to spoil me by letting me do my two favorite things, eating and sleeping. I also chase birds. I HATE dogs. I lead a very carefree life on the roof of our house in California, and I am glad that I was born to be who I am.

I would love to find out about you. What is your name and what do you look like? Where do you live and what are your favorite free-time activities? Who takes care of you? Are you happy? Please write back and tell me about yourself. I am looking forward to your reply.

Your Friend,

Russell

Display the letter on a wall chart. The chart should point out the major components of a "friendly" letter—i.e., date, greeting, body, closing, and name. In a whole group session, explain to the class that when they work in pairs during their computer time, they will need to find this letter on the text disk.

Have a volunteer boot the WA-SYS: Disk and select option 1. After inserting the WA-TEXT: Disk as requested (for a single drive system only), the student next enters his or her name and presses RETURN. The user will be asked:

What text do you want
to work on?

Press ? to see a menu of available text files on the WA-TEXT: Disk. The file FRIENDLY.TEXT should appear. By pressing the letter in the menu corresponding to this text file, the volunteer will load the example letter into *The Writer's Assistant*.

Once the letter has been loaded, other students can try to make the changes in the text (*see* Blackline Master 19 in Appendix for suggestions). Selected changes can be listed on a task card and displayed near the computer screen.

Demonstrate how to change characters and words using the Drop and In commands. First press D (for Drop); then press the RIGHT ARROW or the SPACEBAR key to remove unwanted words. After the characters have been removed from the screen, press CTRL-C. Review the procedures for inserting new characters and words using the In command (*see* Activity 5.2). After you press I (for In), the right side of the line "moves over" to allow the entry of new words. Press CTRL-C to lock in the new text. Have volunteers make each of the requested changes; the class and the teacher can help out when needed. When all the changes have been entered, press Q (for Quit) and U (for Update).

Assign the task of entering the requested changes in the FRIENDLY.TEXT file during scheduled computer time. Students may need more than one session to gain facility with the Drop and In commands. Notice that each student pair will be working with the version of the letter which includes *all* the changes made since you entered it. Because the text may be substantially changed after a few rounds of student editing, it may be necessary to make more than one copy of your original letter and reintroduce the original version from time to time. If you wish to preserve the original letter, students should choose the W (for Write) option after they Quit and rename the file (using their initials) when requested; *see* Activity 5.2 for more information. This option allows each edited file to be saved under a different name rather than replacing the original version.

ACTIVITY 5.4 COMPUTER PAL LETTERS

Objective. To write a friendly letter to a "computer pal" in another classroom

Time Allotment. 30-minute whole group computer session
30-minute computer session for each student pair

Materials.
—Apple II (64K) computer
—*Writer's Assistant* system disk (WA-SYS:)
—Text disk to store students' work (WA-TEXT:)
—Friendly Letter Chart (Blackline Master 18 in Appendix)
—Friendly Letter Task Card (Blackline Master 19 in Appendix)
—Computer Pal Task Card (Blackline Master 20 in Appendix)

PROCEDURE

Early in the school year, contact another computer-using teacher who plans to use the computer to support writing activities. Both classrooms will need to have access to the same (or compatible) computer and word processing systems in order to facilitate the exchange of text disks. Your local Computer Using Educators (CUE) or similar professional organizations may be helpful in locating other interested teachers in your area.

Once you make a teacher contact at your own school, across town, or in another state, introduce your students to the idea of exchanging "computer pal" letters on disk. Ask how many students have had a pen pal before, and discuss the kinds of information generally shared between pen pals. Have a volunteer list on a wall chart the types of information students have exchanged in the past. Try to generate a list of information that might go in a computer pal letter, including possible questions that the letter writers might ask each other. Students usually want information about sports played, daily schedule, favorite TV shows, places traveled, family members, pets and hobbies, and so forth.

Review the letter from Activity 5.3, naming the parts of a friendly letter. Explain that in their first computer pal letter, students might want to include a description of (1) themselves, (2) their interests, and (3) their families. They might also want to include questions for their computer pal (*see* Blackline Master 20 in Appendix).

Finally, review the word processing procedures described in the previous activities—booting the WA-SYS: Disk, selecting option 1, inserting the WA-TEXT: Disk, naming the text (letter) with initials, and using In and Drop commands to write letters. If a printer is available, make two printouts (one to keep and one to send). Place a "mailbox" folder near the computer to store the printed version of the letters in case something happens to the disk.

During scheduled computer time, have each pair of students write a friendly letter to an anonymous computer pal. You may find it more efficient to have novice writers complete a first draft of the letter using pencil and paper. After everyone has entered his/her letter, wrap the disk in heavy cardboard and insert it in an envelope for mailing. When

a disk full of letters comes back from the other computer-using classroom, students can send their responses to individual computer pals.

ACTIVITY 5.5 EDITING A BUSINESS LETTER

Objective. To learn the proper format of a business letter and practice using the editing commands

Time Allotment. 30-minute whole group computer session 30-minute computer session for each student pair

Materials.
—Apple II (64K) computer
—*Writer's Assistant* system disk (WA-SYS:)
—Text disk with previously saved business letter (WA-TEXT:)
—Editing Command Chart (Blackline Master 16 in Appendix)
—Business Letter Chart (Blackline Master 21 in Appendix)
—Business Letter Task Card (Blackline Master 22 in Appendix)

PROCEDURE

Prior to the start of the lesson, enter the following letter under the file name BUSINESS.TEXT, and—using *The Writer's Assistant*—save it on the WA-TEXT: Disk.

Lion Obedience School
100 Park Avenue
San Diego, CA 92093
USA
February 12, 1986

Whiskas Cat Food Company
14876 Feline Avenue
Sydney, New South Wales
Australia 6447

Dear Sir:

While I was living in Papua New Guinea a few years back, I regularly enjoyed your brand of canned cuisine imported from Australia. I looked forward to many years of pleasant dining until one day my owner packed me in a small cage and flew me to California to live. Ever since my arrival, I have been yearning for a can of your rare and wonderful food, but I can't find it anywhere. My owner tries to convince me to accept a substitute "generic brand" cat food, but I continue to hold out for the "original."

Can you help me please? Do you have an importer for your products in this country? Please forward a list of suppliers in my area. Your quick and speedy reply will be much appreciated.

Sincerely,

Russell

In a whole group setting, review the format for both friendly and business letters. Discuss the purpose of each type of letter and the circumstances in which each is appropriate.

> *Friendly Letter*—informal sharing of information with a computer pal, family member, or friend.

> *Business Letter*— formal communication with a company or individual when making a complaint, requesting information, ordering a product, or applying for a job.

Go over the chart (*see* Blackline Master 21 in Appendix) that shows the parts of a business letter (heading, inside address, greeting, body, closing, signature). Review the procedures for booting the WA-SYS: Disk and inserting the WA-TEXT: Disk. Demonstrate how to locate BUSINESS.TEXT and review the In, Drop, and Quit commands. Make a task card listing several editing changes for students to make in BUSINESS.TEXT (*see* Black Linc Master 22 in Appendix).

These are just a few ideas to get started. In addition, you may wish to incorporate grammar lessons by asking students to replace all the singular nouns with plural nouns, put an adjective in front of every noun, or rewrite the letter in the third person.

During scheduled computer time, have each pair of students complete the changes indicated on the task card. Remember that when each student pair Quits and Updates, the previous version of BUSINESS.TEXT will be replaced by the edited version. The next pair of students will subsequently make changes in the text and destroy the version of the letter they found. If students wish to save their edited business letter, they should press W (for Write) after they press Q (for Quit) and rename their text using their initials. Their letter will be saved under the name: [INITIALS].TEXT.

ACTIVITY 5.6 WRITING A BUSINESS LETTER

Objective. To write a business letter requesting information or free materials

Time Allotment. 30-minute whole group session
30-minute computer session for each computer pair

Materials.
—Apple II (64K) computer
—*Writer's Assistant* system disk (WA-SYS:)
—Text disk to store students' work (WA-TEXT:)
—Business Letter Chart (Blackline Master 21 in Appendix)
—Request Letter Chart (Blackline Master 23 in Appendix)
—Envelope Chart (Blackline Master 24 in Appendix)
—Addresses of places to write
—Envelopes

PROCEDURE

In a whole group session, review the format and purposes of a business letter. Explain that during their computer time, each pair of students will write a business letter to the company of their choice. You may wish to correlate this activity with a current social studies or science theme. The two books listed below offer a wide range of sources to contact for free materials and information:

1. *The Kid's Whole Future Catalog*
   By Paula Taylor
   New York: Random House, 1982.

2. *Free Stuff For Kids*
   Edited by Louise Delagran
   Deephaven, MN: Meadowbrook Press, 1983.

Students may find guidelines for writing business letters, displayed on a poster, useful as a reference when they write their business letters; *see* Blackline Master 23 in Appendix.

Quickly review the procedures for using *The Writer's Assistant* (WA-SYS:) and the text disk (WA-TEXT:). By this time, most students should require little assistance in booting the system and entering their letters. This activity requires access to a printer in order to send the letters to the various businesses. Have each student pair select an item to request, write an appropriate letter during their regular computer time, and print two copies of their letter. The students should correctly address the envelope in ink (*see* Blackline Master 22 in Appendix); sign, fold, and insert the letter; and put it in the "mailbox" folder for the teacher to review and mail.

Writing Poetry

No writing curriculum would be complete without poetry. Poetry is an ideal medium for writing instruction in that it helps students express themselves in a rich yet condensed format. It focuses on economy of text and in its rhythm demonstrates the potential strength of language. Often, poetry requires a specific structure or pattern which further develops the discipline of the writer.

Many forms of poetry make excellent teaching activities for the elementary grades; the couplet, cinquain, senryu, and limerick all work well. Haiku, a traditional Japanese form of poetry, is a particularly popular form for introducing youngsters to the power of poetic expression. Highly structured, brief, and not requiring forced rhyming, the haiku form often produces moving and impressive verse, an important consideration when trying to encourage young writers. It is, moreover, a form of poetry which relies on nature as its source of motivation, something common to the experience of us all.

While some may see a conflict in using a computer to create something as delicate as a poem, we do not. We chose to integrate the teaching of haiku poetry, facilitated through the use of computer software, as a way to introduce the six-step writing pro-

By Barbara Miller-Souviney and Randall Souviney

cess described in Chapter 3. The structured nature of haiku makes it relatively easy to create computer-generated "writing prompts." We have found that using well-designed software as a component in the writing process can substantially reduce the difficulty some young writers experience with poetic expression.

The use of the writing process enhances—as it does with other styles of writing—both the experience of writing poetry and the quality of the final product. In haiku writing, the response and revision phases of the writing process are particularly important due to the subtle nature of the phrasing in this form of poetry.

General Overview

Students engage in the following stages of the writing process when creating a haiku poem:

1. Pre-writing—brainstroming ideas before writing
2. Writing—composing the first draft of text
3. Response—feedback provided by peers on each composition
4. Revision—making corrections and editing final draft

5. Evaluation—reviewing final draft according to objective
6. Post-writing—sharing and display of final composition

Children should work with a partner when composing their haiku poem on the computer. The objective is to create an original haiku poem which expresses a perception about a single aspect of nature—e.g., a season of the year. Each of the three lines must adhere to the following syllable count:

Line 1—5 syllables
Line 2—7 syllables
Line 3—5 syllables

Two brown logs burning
Ice gripping the window tight
Cold wind speaking low

After completing the series of activities in Chapter 6, students should be able to:

1. Describe the structure of a haiku poem
2. Write a haiku poem for display in the classroom
3. Utilize the six steps of the writing process to create orignal poetry

ACTIVITY 6.1
HAIKU PRE-WRITING

Objective.   To understand the structure of a haiku poem and to develop ideas for writing a haiku poem

Time Allotment.   45-minute whole group session

Materials.   —Pictures of nature and seasons (magazine pictures and posters work well)
—Written examples of haiku poems (Blackline Master 25 in Appendix)
—Butcher paper for recording ideas

PROCEDURE

In a whole group session, show pictures of the four seasons. Ask the students to describe each picture by giving as many details as possible. Probe by asking questions about personal activities during each season such as how the weather might feel or places of interest to students. As the class generates ideas, have one child write words on butcher paper for later use during the clustering and writing activities. Make four columns on the butcher paper—"Fall," "Winter," "Spring," "Summer"—to help organize the ideas as they are generated.

Materials. —Poster and follow-up materials from previous activity
—Paper and pencils

PROCEDURE

Review the previous activity in a whole group session. Remind students about the four seasons, the wall chart containing descriptive words about the four seasons, and the sample haiku poems. Invite the students to read the poems out loud and clap out the syllables. Write the numbers 5, 7, 5 on the board as a reminder.

Now have the students meet with their computer partners to brainstorm ideas about the haiku that they will be writing on the computer. Encourage each pair to agree on a season to describe and to cluster their ideas at the top of a sheet of paper. Each pair should then compose a haiku poem together and write it on paper. Expect to hear some quiet hand clapping and see some finger counting during this time. Have the students keep their poems for later entry during each pair's scheduled computer time.

Read several examples of haiku poems and explain that they are special poems which describe nature creatively. A haiku poem has three lines: the first line has five syllables; the second line has seven syllables; and the third line has five syllables. Have the children clap out each syllable to help them remember the 5, 7, 5 pattern of the three lines.

As a homework assignment, ask the children to choose a season they would like to describe in a haiku poem. Have them write a list of descriptive words that they might use when writing their poems. They can refer to the words listed on the butcher paper chart or ask their parents for suggestions. Tell them that during the next day's lesson, they will meet with their computer partners to discuss their ideas, write one or more haiku poems, and enter their creations on the computer when it is their turn.

ACTIVITY 6.2
CLUSTERING IDEAS
FOR HAIKU

Objective. To select descriptive words and cluster ideas in preparation for writing haiku poems

Time Allotment. 10-minute whole group session
30-minute session working in pairs

Nature Words	Weather Words	Games of the Season
leaves snow sun soil tree flower animal breeze bird field	tornado rain snow fog cloud hail wind sleet storm	football soccer basketball lacrosse

ACTIVITY 6.3
WRITING HAIKU POEMS

Objective. To enter one or more haiku poems into the computer

Time Allotment. 30-minute computer session for each student pair for one or two weeks

Materials.
—Apple II (64K) computer
—Printer
—*Poetry Writing Tool* or *The Writer's Assistant* and Text Disk (EBE Corp.)
—Haiku Poem Chart (Blackline Master 25 in Appendix)
—Examples of haiku poems

PROCEDURE

Devise a computer-use schedule so that all students have the opportunity to write haiku poems using a word processor or the *Poetry Writing Tool* (EBE Corp.). Scheduling children in pairs works well if only one computer is available. Thirty-minute blocks are generally adequate to compose at least one haiku poem (*see* Blackline Master 25 in Appendix). Working in pairs, students should use their clustered ideas from the previous lesson to compose one or more haiku poems on the computer. Prompted writing tools like the *Poetry Writing Tool* can provide on-screen support by supplying key questions and suggestions. If time allows, students may enter their previously written poems as well. Copies of finished poems can be saved on disk and printed for use in the response and revision stages of the writing process. Each pair of students should print three copies, one for themselves, one for the response group, and one to be filed.

ACTIVITY 6.4
HAIKU RESPONSE

Objective. To suggest changes and improvements in each other's poems

Time Allotment.   30-minute whole group session
Two 30-minute sessions working in pairs

Materials.   —Printed haiku poems from previous activity
—Dictionaries
—Pencils

PROCEDURE

In a whole group session, ask for volunteers to read their poems out loud to the class. Ask the class to think about possible changes while listening to the poems. Stress that both positive responses and constructive criticism are welcome. Remind them that the purpose of response is to help each other write the best possible haiku poems. An informal and friendly atmosphere will encourage the children to share their work and use the comments to improve their writing.

Next, demonstrate a few examples of editing on the board: e.g., reword an awkward phrase, correct the syllable count in a line, correct spelling and punctuation, select a new title. This is also a good time to emphasize that responses from other writers can help authors improve their work.

Write one of the poems on the board (without identifying the student pair who wrote it), or make up a poem with several errors. Have the students identify errors and suggest improvements while you make the corrections on the board. Encourage the use of dictionaries during this process. Students should see that their responsibility as editors includes correcting errors as well as offering general comments designed to help the writer make revisions.

During a second session, form response groups of four or five students. A response group works together to make comments and write corrections on each poem. Each student pair will later use these comments to change their text on the computer. If time allows, it may be useful to schedule two response sessions—one to look only at possible im-provements in the poem (descriptive words, title, etc.) and a second session to fix errors in spelling, punctuation, and grammar.

ACTIVITY 6.5 HAIKU REVISION

Objective.   To revise the haiku poems using response group comments

Time Allotment.   30-minute computer session for each student pair

Materials. —Apple II (64K) computer
—Printer
—*The Writer's Assistant* (WA-SYS:)
—Text disk with original poems (WA-TEXT:)
—Edited haiku poems

PROCEDURE

During scheduled times, pairs of students revise their poem(s) on the computer. Explain that each pair should load their original haiku poem from the text disk and make any changes they wish based on the comments from the response group. Leave the folder of edited poems on the computer stand so that students can refer to them as required. Make clear to all the students that they are not obligated to make the suggested changes. Authors make the final decisions about their work.

Again, students should print three copies of their work, one for the teacher and one for each student. If appropriate, the teacher and/or peers can evaluate each pair's revised poem(s).

ACTIVITY 6.6 EVALUATING HAIKU POEMS

Objective. To assess each haiku poem

Time Allotment. 30-minute small group session

Materials. —Printouts of edited haiku poems

PROCEDURE

The primary responsibility for assessment of student work usually belongs to the teacher. Students, however, can take over some of this responsibility. One way to involve students in this process is to form a committee (similar to the classroom editorial board described in Activity 8.8) which is responsible for evaluating each poem. The committee should discuss criteria for evaluation such as correct form and syllabication, appropriate title and content, and effective use of words and details.

Divide the students into several groups, and distribute the haiku poems written by other members of the class. Everyone should have an opportunity to serve on an evaluation committee.

ACTIVITY 6.7
SHARING HAIKU POEMS

Objective. To display final versions of haiku poems for public viewing

Time Allotment. 45-minute session working in pairs

Materials. —Printouts of haiku poems
—Paints, crayons, art paper

PROCEDURE

It is important for authors to know that their writing will be displayed for people to read. There are several ways this can be accomplished. Try displaying the poems in school hallways, the library, school office, or on a classroom bulletin board. Utilizing a variety of art materials, students can illustrate their poems by depicting in picture form what they have attempted to capture in words. After they complete their pictures, students can cut out and attach their poems. When the time comes to replace the poems with other writing, put the haiku poems in a class book to be kept in the class library.

Here is one example, called a Poet-Tree, of a way to display students' work:

POET-TREE

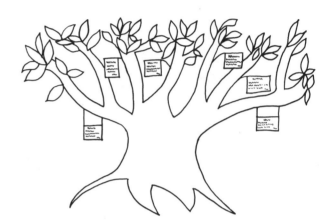

Expository Writing

Nearly everyone, at some time, needs to write instructions for an event or activity, lesson plans, repair manuals, catalog descriptions, recipes, etc. Because this form of writing is fairly straight forward and easy to evaluate, it should be included in an elementary writing program.

The computer can be used effectively to assist students to learn to write clear, concise expository compositions. Each of the four activities in this chapter gives students an expository writing task to complete. In the first activity, students make a selection from several phrases at each stage of making a sandwich. The computer provides all the text and organization while the student determines the direction of the plot. In the following four software-supported activities, the student gradually takes over more of the responsibility for paragraph organization and text entry (*see* Chapters 2 and 3). In each of these activities, moreover, the writer produces a complete first draft of an expository composition as one component in the writing process.

General Overview

In expository writing, the author attempts to de-

By Barbara Miller-Souviney and Randall Souviney

scribe an event or procedure to be carried out by the reader. Generally, an expository composition is structured as follows:

1. An introduction gives an overview of the task or procedure to be described.
2. A main paragraph describes the steps needed to complete the specified activity.
3. A conclusion tells how the writer feels upon completing the activity or the writer's reflections on the process involved.

The following set of four activities makes use of interactive writing software called the *Expository Writing Tool* (Encyclopaedia Britannica Educational Corporation). Each of these activities can be used for one cycle of student computer use (about one week). During a second one-week cycle, the output files saved on text disks can be edited using a word processor. This two-week cycle (one week to write and one to edit) is a common pattern. Response groups can be formed between the writing and editing cycles.

In each of the four activities, students produce a piece of expository writing with varying amounts of support from the computer. The programs are designed to be used in sequence so that students take on more responsibility for producing text as they gain experience. By participating in the production of good models of expository text, children learn to write on their own.

Each of these four expository writing activities can be used as a component in the writing process. First, place all the completed printouts of an activity in a folder. Next, read a sample of the stories to the class, or, if time allows, invite students to read their own stories. Then, form response groups to make suggestions and corrections on the printed copies. As the editing cycle begins, encourage students to use their edited printouts when making changes in textfiles. Finally, make new printouts and display the final versions on bulletin boards or place them into a class book.

After completing the series of activities in Chapter 7, students should be able to:

1. Write an original expository composition that has a title, introduction, body, and conclusion
2. Use a word processor to edit and print an expository composition as one component in the writing process

ACTIVITY 7.1 SANDWICH MAKING

Objective. To create an expository composition with maximum support provided by the computer

Time Allotment. 45-minute whole group session
30-minute computer session working in pairs

Materials. —Apple II (64K) computer
—Printer
—"Sandwich Making"

program (*Expository Writing Tool*)
—Expository Poster (Blackline Master 26 in Appendix)

PROCEDURE

In a whole group session, introduce the "Sandwich Making" program to the students. Discuss the purpose of expository writing and the structure of a good expository text. Explain that the author describes how something is constructed or the steps in a procedure. As an example, demonstrate how the computer program helps the user to write the directions for making a sandwich. Point out that the students will need to make selections that the computer program gives them for their sandwich ingredients.

Read the computer program's directions out loud as you show the directions on the screen. Write one story together, asking volunteers from the class to give choices for the ingredients. The children will probably want to go on and on, writing the longest set of instructions possible. At some point, however, choose to add no more ingredients, thereby ending the story. Print the story, and have a student read it out loud. Point out the three parts of the story—introduction, body, and conclusion—and emphasize the importance of all three parts in an expository composition (*see* Blackline Master 26 in Appendix).

Expository Composition

1. Title: Name for your composition
2. By: Type your name
3. Introductory Paragraph: Main idea(s)—tell why you are writing about the subject
4. Body: Give details that support your main idea(s)
5. Conclusion: Tell how you feel when you finish the activity or why you will—or won't—do it again

Allow the children to use "Sandwich Making"

during their computer time that week. Students should save their stories on text disks and print three copies. Use these printouts during response groups and the editing session the following week.

ACTIVITY 7.2 OUR SCHOOL DAY

Objective. To write the sequence of events that makes up a typical school day

Time Allotment. 45-minute whole group session

30-minute computer session working in pairs

Materials. —Apple II (64K) computer
—Printer
—"Our School Day" program (*Expository Writing Tool*)
—Expository Poster (Blackline Master 26 in Appendix)

PROCEDURE

Explain to the students that they will be writing an expository composition about their typical school-day schedules. The program will give them the structure of the story by providing the introduction, body, and conclusion along with much of the text. The students will need to fill in words or finish sentences to complete their expository stories.

Go through the activity with the students, reading the text presented aloud. Take suggestions from the group to complete each segment of the story, discussing other possible ways to fill in words or complete sentences. Finally, print the class story and have a student read it. Ask students to listen for the introduction, body, and conclusion and to describe the contents of each part. Review the poster describing the parts of an expository composition (Blackline Master 26 in Appendix), and display it near the computer for student reference.

This activity is likely to take two weeks. Use the same procedure described earlier in the chapter for this two-week cycle.

ACTIVITY 7.3 HOW A COMPUTER WORKS

Objective. To write a composition about the successful operation of a computer

Time Allotment. 45-minute whole group session
30-minute computer session working in pairs

Materials. —Apple II (64K) computer
—Printer
—"How A Computer Works" program (*Expository Writing Tool*)
—Expository Poster (Blackline Master 26 in Appendix)

PROCEDURE

In a whole group session, ask your students to describe how they operate the classroom computer.

After some discussion, ask the students if this task could be an example of expository writing. Have a student describe out loud the steps required for operating a computer. See if the class can identify the three components of an expository composition.

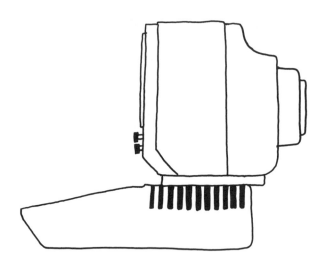

Introduce the program "How A Computer Works." Again, pairs of students will write a story with the help of the computer, but this time the computer will provide less support than in the previous two activities. The computer will provide the introduction and conclusion, but the students must actually write the steps required to operate a computer successfully. Although this second paragraph—the body—includes topic sentences to help students organize their ideas, the students must fill in the actual steps and details.

Try the program with the whole group working together to create a class version of how to run a computer. Depending on your class, the students may feel comfortable enough to talk through possibilities. Be sure to emphasize that because their composition may be read by someone who has never used a computer before, it is important to think through the sequence of instructions carefully before they write. Sharing completed stories with a group lacking computer experience may be a real motivation for the students to write clearly and to show off their expertise. A younger or less experienced class at your school may be just the place to display your students' expository compositions.

Follow the same cycle of writing, response groups, and editing described in the previous activities.

ACTIVITY 7.4 HOW TO

Objective. To write an expository story, with very little computer

support, about how to do some job or activity

Time Allotment. 45-minute whole group session
30-minute computer session working in pairs

Materials.
—Apple II (64K) computer
—Printer
—"How To" program (*Expository Writing Tool*)
—Expository Poster (Blackline Master 26 in Appendix)

PROCEDURE

In a whole group session, ask the children to define the word "advice." Once the group has established

a definition, explain that in this expository writing activity, the computer will only give advice or suggestions as the students compose an original expository composition on a topic of their own choosing.

Brainstorm topics to write about, or review suggestions contained within the program. Demonstrate the "How To" program, and point out the type of advice it provides. Authors must organize and enter all of the text for the entire story. Point out that they should use the same three-part composition structure they used in the previous three activities.

As students complete stories during their computer time, they should make three printouts for use during response groups and the editing cycle. All the expository stories can be bound into a class book or displayed on school bulletin boards. Some may be appropriate for inclusion in a class newspaper.

Classroom Newspapers and Networks

The activities in this chapter serve as a plan for introducing skills specific to newspaper writing and for applying those skills to the production of a classroom newspaper using a word processing program. Developing classroom newspapers can provide a year-long opportunity for students to engage in the writing process.

Students invest more effort in their writing when they know other people will read it. News networks between nearby schools or established networks such as *The InterLearn Newswire Network* (InterLearn) can be used to expand the audience for which students are writing. Writing to students in different locations helps children to understand the need for vivid description and explicit detail when describing events they might otherwise take for granted.

While student work can be transmitted electronically between computers, it is also possible to create networks by sharing information stored on disks which can be exchanged through the mail. The means of transmission is not as important as the form of the information when it is received. Ideally, the information is received in a form that can be easily revised and printed in the same format as locally produced stories. Reviewing articles written by students from other schools and serving on "editorial boards" that prepare articles for inclusion in a local newspaper often help reluctant students expand their writing interests.

General Overview

Writing for a newspaper involves a range of writing skills. Students can employ descriptive, expository, and other forms of writing when preparing articles for publication. Student journalists are required to provide factual coverage of information and sequential descriptions of events in their reporting. A good newspaper article generally includes facts about each of the "5 W's":

Who—include the names of those involved
What—describe what happened
Where—where did the event take place
When—when did it happen
Why—what were the reasons for the event

Teaching writing in this way gives students a purpose for writing and provides a "real" audience. Professional news offices today use word processing

*By Kim Whooley, Randall Souviney,
and Margaret M. Riel*

technology and computer networks to produce daily newspapers. Students can take advantage of the same computer technology to produce a classroom newspaper.

Working on a classroom newspaper is an activity that helps students understand writing as a process. The following activities are arranged to help students in each of the writing stages.

Steps in the Writing Process

Pre-Writing—Discuss current events, review newspaper articles written by others, conduct brainstorming sessions.

Writing—Students write their first draft of an article using a prompted writing environment or word processor.

Response—Students share what they have written with their peers, discuss strengths and weaknesses, and suggest ideas for improvements.

Revision—Students edit their work, making corrections and producing a final draft.

Evaluation—Final drafts are reviewed in small groups of 4-6 students who assess the content and form of the story, making final decisions about which articles to publish in their newspaper.

Post-Writing—Newspapers are assembled, produced, and distributed to class members, others in the school, and student reporters from other classrooms whose stories were included.

Many of the following activities are based on software called *Computer Chronicles: The News Writing Tool* (Encyclopaedia Britannica Educational Corporation). This interactive tool provides on-screen prompting for writing articles that are appropriate to the various sections of a classroom newspaper. The program helps students isolate the type of story they are going to write, and it provides specific information or guidance on writing the type of article selected. *QUILL Planners* can be written to provide similar guidance within the *QUILL* sys-

tem. Although any word processor can be used for these activities, it might be necessary to provide some additional guidance for the pre-writing and writing stages in the form of task cards.

The activities in this chapter assume access to an Apple II (64K) computer with a disk drive and a printer. After completing the series of activities in Chapter 8, students should be able to:

1. Understand the different types of articles that are found in sections of a newspaper
2. Write a news article that includes the key elements—who, what, where, when, and why
3. Participate on an editorial board that selects and edits articles and to assist with the production of a classroom newspaper

The task for each group is to find at least one article from each of the listed sections, cut it out, and paste it on a piece of construction paper with corresponding heading. Allow about 10 minutes for this part of the activity. When the class is finished, discuss any additional sections discovered and add them to the class list on the board. Have a person from each group read an article selected by the group. Each group must present an article from a *different* section. If time allows, discuss the articles briefly by reviewing who, what, why, when, and where questions. You can use the article posters as the beginning of a current events scrapbook.

ACTIVITY 8.1 PARTS OF A NEWSPAPER

Objective.   To introduce the parts of a newspaper and components of an effective article

Time Allotment.   30-minute small group session

Materials.   —Multiple copies of same edition of newspaper
—Scissors
—Paste
—Markers or crayons
—Construction paper

PROCEDURE

Have the groups of four to five students list as many sections of a newspaper as they can. After a few minutes, have one student from each group read the group's list, and compile a class list on the board. Then, give each group copies of the same newspaper along with scissors, paste, markers, and construction paper.

ACTIVITY 8.2 CURRENT EVENTS REPORTING

Objective.   To learn to select articles of interest from a newspaper, summarize the articles, and report orally to classmates

Time Allotment.   10-15 minutes daily

Materials.   —Network sign
—Microphone
—World map
—Typewriter

PROCEDURE

Ask the students if they watch news broadcasts. Have them name the anchor persons they watch. Discuss what these people do, and explain that students will take turns being anchor persons for a classroom television station.

Set up a weekly rotating schedule so that each student has an opportunity to report once a week (4-5 students per day). Ask the students to select articles of interest from their home newspapers, and explain that they must summarize the information in the articles, paying attention to who, what, why, when, and where questions. It may be necessary to bring in a newspaper each morning for students who may not have access to one. The news clippings from which students prepare their summaries should be dated and collected in a news scrapbook for later use at a writing center.

Set up a "newsroom desk" with the necessary props (microphone, network sign, typewriter, world map) that the students will use when presenting their news. Encourage students to watch news programs and imitate the formats that they see. Students often find it fun to use "stage names" as well.

The news should be "broadcast" at about the same time each day. These regular broadcasts may also be used to incorporate student-prepared commercials (. . . and now a word from our sponsor) and other broadcast activities such as book reviews and editorials. Later in the year, an occasional audio or video recording may add motivation.

ACTIVITY 8.3 NEWSPAPER SCRAPBOOK CENTER

Objective.   To have students read, summarize, and comment on current events and locate specified areas on a map

Time Allotment.   10-minute whole group introductory session
25-minute session for each student pair for one week

Materials.   —Current event scrapbook
—World maps (8x10 sheets and wall size)
—Paper and pencil (word processor or typewriter may be substituted)

—News Chart Center
(Blackline Master 27 in
Appendix)

PROCEDURE

In a brief whole group session early in the week, introduce the newspaper scrapbook center. Pairs of students should be scheduled to work at the center independently. Write the following instructions on a chart and display it at the center:

NEWS CENTER

- Select an article which interests you from the scrapbook.

- Read the article very carefully.

- Write a summary without looking at it again. Remember
  WHO ?   WHERE ?
  WHAT?   WHEN ?
  WHY ?
  If you can't remember, look again !

- Write a comment or opinion about the article. What do you think ?

- Find the location of the event on the wall map. Label it on the small map.

- Staple the map to your summary. Put your completed paper in the folder for others to read.

- Read what others have written. Read the scrapbook.

This activity may be repeated periodically, or special interest scrapbooks (Olympics, Presidential elections) may be compiled for added motivation.

ACTIVITY 8.4 COMPUTER NEWS NETWORKS

Objective. To introduce the idea of "news networks" in the production of a classroom newspaper

Time Allotment. 30-minute whole group session

Materials.
—Newspaper with AP or UPI stories
—*Computer Chronicles: The News Writing Tool* or *QUILL Planner* or any word processor
—U.S. and world maps
—Classroom newspapers from other schools
—Disk for mailing articles to other classrooms
—Press cards

PROCEDURE

In a whole group session, discuss the purpose of newswires. Display the front page of the local newspaper, and ask the students to describe the parts (headlines, table of contents, pictures, captions, masthead) and why each is important. Discuss who writes the articles in the newspaper and where the paper is printed.

Next, point out a story written about a distant country (show its location on the map). Ask the students to name the person who wrote the article, and discuss how the news travels from the place where the event occurs to the place where the newspaper is printed. Some students may know that computers are involved in the transmission; others may suggest that reporters fly back and forth or phone in stories. Discuss how the computer speeds up communication by allowing reporters to transmit articles and even photographs over the phone lines.

Show a copy of a classroom newspaper from another school. Discuss the articles and who wrote them. Ask about how stories from different places were collected. Explain that by using compatible computers, students from any class—even from other countries—can send stories on disk to another classroom where the stories can be read on the computer screen, edited using a word processor, and printed. Explain that the class will be evaluating stories from other classrooms, as well as locally written articles, for inclusion in their own newspaper.

Demonstrate the *Computer Chronicles* (or teacher-prepared task cards and any word processor) so that students understand how it can help them write their own articles on the computer. Tell them that their stories will also be sent to other schools for possible inclusion in local newspapers. Pass out the student press cards and discuss possible uses (e.g., getting into the dugout for an interview with the little league coach).

ACTIVITY 8.5 PREPARING TO WRITE NEWS ARTICLES

Objective.   To have students report the factual details of an event they have experienced

Time Allotment.   15-minute whole group discussion
30-minute individual writing session

Materials.   —Photos (if possible) from a shared experience such as a field trip, school or class event, film, activity, game, etc.

PROCEDURE

As a pre-writing activity, have the students discuss an event in which the whole class participated. Discuss who participated, the purpose of the event, where it was, when it was, what happened, etc. Write the facts on the board as the students present them. Discuss the "voice" of a newspaper—i.e., a non-participant observing and recording the activity. Have a volunteer try to describe the event in a "reporter's voice." For example:

> Ms. Brown's class went on a field trip. The students traveled by bus to the museum, and several of the students . . . .

Have each student (or pair of students) write an outline of an article which covers Ms. Brown's field trip or a real experience each has had.

ACTIVITY 8.6 WRITING NEWS ARTICLES

Objective. To produce a newspaper article using a computer and appropriate software

Time Allotment. 30-minute computer session working in pairs

Materials.
—Apple II (64K) computer
—Printer
—*Computer Chronicles: News Writing Tool* or *QUILL Planner* (or word processor with task cards)
—*The InterLearn Newswire Network* (InterLearn)
—Charts (Blackline Masters 28 and 29 in Appendix)

PROCEDURE

Previous pre-writing activities have prepared students to write news articles. Schedule students into the computer center in pairs to write their articles using posted and/or screen-displayed directions (*Computer Chronicles*). If the *Computer Chronicles: News Writing Tool* software is not available, use *The Writer's Assistant*, the *QUILL Planner*, the *Bank Street Writer*, *Apple Works*, or another word processor together with teacher-made task cards posted near the center.

The number of writing and editing sessions will vary according to student skills and experience. Depending on the amount of computer time available, some teachers have found scheduling easier if students do their pre-writing and first drafts of their articles off the computer. If time does not allow every student pair to compose articles at the computer, they can quickly enter previously written ar-

ticles during their scheduled computer time or after school, editing and reformatting as necessary.

COMPUTER CHRONICLES: NEWS WRITING TOOL
Garrison Bureau

Welcome Cub Reporters!

This week is get acquainted week. These directions will help you to use the *Computer Chronicles: News Writing Tool* disk and let you practice storing text for future editing. Enjoy the exploration and experimentation!

The Field Editor

ACTIVITY 8.7 RESPONSE TO NEWS ARTICLES

Objective. To introduce the idea of response groups for providing feedback to authors on how to improve their articles

Time Allotment.   30-minute whole group session
30-minute session working in pairs

Materials.   —Printed copies of news articles from Activity 8.6
—Editing Codes Chart (Blackline Master 30 in Appendix)
—Editing Checklist (Blackline Master 31 in Appendix)
—Dictionaries
—Pencils, pens

EDITING CODES

∧   (caret) means something has been left out

Ø   slash through a capital letter means make it lower case

r̲̲̲   three lines under a lower case letter means make it a capital

(sp)   circled sp above a word means the word is misspelled

₱   double lined P means make a new paragraph

✳   (asterisk) means to look at the note at the bottom of the page

PROCEDURE

Response groups can be an effective way to give feedback to students who then use this feedback to improve their articles. Ask the class questions like the following:

1. What information should be included in a good news article? (5 W's)

2. How should the article be organized? (introduction, body, conclusion)

3. What rules of grammar should be followed in writing? (punctuation, verb tense, noun/verb agreement, etc.)

Summarize the students' responses to these questions on the board. Explain that when authors are writing down ideas during brainstorming sessions, they often are unable to accomplish all of these goals. Generally, they need to edit their writing. Discuss the types of skills an editor must have. Ask why authors might want to ask someone else to edit their work rather than editing it themselves. Explain that the class will be working in pairs to make suggestions for improving the content, organization, grammar, and punctuation of each others' articles.

Emphasize that the final decisions regarding changes rest with the author. Suggestions can be given orally, or partners can write suggestions directly on printed copies of the articles. The class may want to use standard codes for indicating corrections—e.g., "P" means new paragraph, "sp" means spelling error.

Divide the class into pairs. Give each student pair a printed copy of the article that one of the pair wrote during Activity 8.6. If the students wrote in pairs, there should be just enough articles for each editing pair. If every member of the class wrote an article, each editing pair should work on both articles.

Have students review the standards they developed for good newspaper writing, rules of punctuation, grammar, and spelling. Remind students that the author of the article has the final say regarding changes and corrections. Editing pairs should then read the article(s) and note the corrections and changes agreed upon. The team should discuss its suggestions for changes and be prepared to support its editorial alterations by citing specific improvements in content, organization, and language mechanics.

Once authors are satisfied with the form and content of their work, they should use the word processor to enter changes during regularly scheduled computer time. Encourage students to share their completed final drafts with the entire class as a way of validating the importance of the editorial effort.

ACTIVITY 8.8 REVISING NEWS ARTICLES

Objective. To edit newspaper articles using a word processor

Time Allotment. 30-minute computer session working in pairs

Materials.
—Printed copies of news articles from Activity 8.6
—*The Writer's Assistant* and Text Disk
—Editing Codes (Blackline Master 30 in Appendix)
—Editing Checklist (Blackline Master 31 in Appendix)
—Editing Computer Chronicles Chart (Blackline Master 32 in Appendix)
—Dictionaries, pencils, pens

PROCEDURE

The original author(s) should review changes and corrections offered during the response session and determine which of the alterations to incorporate into the final draft. Authors may make additional changes at this time as well. To encourage further editing (if necessary), it may be advisable for students to submit their completed work to the teacher for a final review.

ACTIVITY 8.9 EDITORIAL BOARD MEETINGS

Objective. To select and prepare articles for inclusion in the local edition of the Computer Chronicles

Time Allotment. 30-minute board meetings daily for about two weeks (meetings may need to occur during lunch or after school)

Materials.
—Printouts of student articles
—Printouts of articles from other classrooms or schools

PROCEDURE

This activity represents the evaluation stage of the writing process. The goal of this activity is for students to create an evaluation framework for determining the quality of student writing to be included in the classroom newspaper. The role of the teacher should be one of facilitator, not decision maker.

Select six to eight students of varying ability levels to serve on the editorial board (all students should serve sometime during the school year). During the first meeting, discuss the need to provide the writer with helpful feedback. Board members should establish standards they wish to set for accepting or rejecting articles for publication. It is important to allow students to arrive at their own set of criteria.

List suggested criteria as they are offered. Among the criteria the board should consider are the following:

1. interesting topic
2. makes sense
3. well written with few editorial errors
4. covers the topic (5 W's)
5. addresses important topic

To minimize subjective decisions, members of the editorial board should understand that they will be responsible for giving the reason for the rejection of an article. Their rationale for rejection should help writers improve future articles.

Board members should read all the submitted articles and determine in which section of the newspaper each article belongs. If some sections have too few articles, it may be necessary to request additional articles. Handwritten articles must be entered on disk and printed.

Distribute the articles from one section of the newspaper to the board members so that each member has at least one article to read. Ask members to read their article silently, making mental notes of their comments. Then have the board members take turns reading the articles aloud to the rest of the board and presenting their evaluations. Encourage students to discuss their reasons for saying an article is "good" or "poor."

Finally, the board must separate the articles into "accept," "reject," and "maybe" folders and make final selections for the newspaper. If they cannot reach unanimous agreement, then a majority vote should decide for or against inclusion. Remind the students that a rejection requires an explanation to the author.

Repeat this process for each section of the newspaper. Members of the editorial board then complete the final editing of the selected articles, using the word processor.

As an alternative method for selecting articles, you may wish to set up an editor's desk center.

Students working in pairs at the center can read and evaluate articles (both local and off the newswire) and complete an evaluation poll. After the entire class has completed the poll, the highest-rated articles are selected for inclusion in the class newspaper. Any student can volunteer to edit the articles that require further work.

THE EDITOR'S DESK

Name Your Favorite

Read the articles from our newswire. Fill in the poll by finding the name of your favorite article and placing a star in the box beside it.

Name of Article												
Cutting Ice	★	★	★									
Fund Raiser	★	★										
Olympics	★	★	★	★	★	★	★	★				
Concert												
Cable TV	★											
School Store	★	★	★	★	★							
Pet Parade	★	★	★	★								
Talent Show												
Fishing	★	★	★	★								
Baskets	★	★	★									
Interview												
Gymnastics	★	★	★	★	★	★	★	★				
Substitute	★	★	★									
Jog A Thon	★	★	★	★	★	★						
Video Game	★	★	★	★								
Review	★	★										

ACTIVITY 8.10 ASSEMBLING THE CLASSROOM NEWSPAPER

Objective. To assemble and distribute copies of the Classroom Computer Chronicles

Time Allotment. Three 45- to 60-minute small group sessions

Materials.
—Final copy of the selected articles
—Artwork
—Header pages
—Rubber cement
—Correction fluid

PROCEDURE

This activity represents the post-writing stage of the writing process. Articles selected by the editorial board must be formatted with the word processor into 40-character column widths and printed. Artwork must be prepared either on the computer—if graphics software is available—or drawn by hand.

Cut out and arrange articles to fill each sheet of header paper, preprinted or hand-lettered with section titles. Once the page layout has been completed, the articles can be "pasted-up." Using rubber cement for the paste-up allows easy repositioning of articles if necessary. Hand-lettered headlines, captions, and artwork can be added at this time. The final paste-up should be examined carefully by the board and then photocopied. Next, use correction fluid to reduce the cut-lines which generally appear around each article, headline, and graphic. Finally, use the clean master to make multiple photocopies, assemble the pages, and distribute the newspaper.

The classroom newspaper can be used as reading material for other lessons. For example, you can have students locate and classify different types of articles (e.g., sports, local and world news, cultural events, etc.). You can also use the articles as a source of spelling words, examples of proper grammatical usage, and vocabulary words. Assess reading comprehension by assigning students to develop several questions about specific articles for the rest of the class to answer. Have students locate and read aloud particularly well-written sentences and paragraphs. Have your class identify articles which would benefit from the inclusion of a picture, and then have them draw appropriate artwork. Share copies of the newspaper with another class or school, and encourage the students who receive the newspaper to submit articles for future publication. Send copies to the principal, the superintendent, the mayor . . . . There really is no limit to the number of follow-up activities that you can create with the Classroom Computer Chronicles.

References

Allan, S. Computers in education: the process of change. Muir Special Project Paper. La Jolla, CA: University of California, San Diego, 1984.

Amarel, M. Classrooms and computers as instructional settings. *Theory Into Practice*, 1983, *22(4)*: 260-272.

Atkinson, R. C. Ingredients for a theory of instruction. *American Psychologist*, 1972, *27*: 921-931.

Bitter, G. The road to computer literacy:.objectives and activities; parts I-IV. *Electronic Learning*, Oct., Nov., Dec., 1982, Jan., Feb., 1983.

Boruta, M., C. Carpenter, M. Harvey, T. Keyser, J. LaBonte, H. Mehan, and D. Rodriguez. Computers in schools: stratifier or equalizer? *The Quarterly Newsletter of the Laboratory of Comparative Human Cognition*, 1983, *5(3)*: 51-55.

Brown, A. and L. French. *The Zone of Proximal Development: Implications for Intelligence Testing for the Year 2000.* University of Illinois: Center for the Study of Reading, 1979.

Bruce, B. C. and A. D. Rubin. What are we learning with QUILL? M. L. Kamie and R. C. Leslie (Eds.). *Perspectives on Computers and Instruction for Reading and Writing.* Rochester, NY: National Reading Conference, 1983.

Cheney, A. *The Reading Corner.* Glenview, IL: Scott, Foresman and Company, 1979.

Cohen, M. Exemplary computer use in education. *Sigcue Bulletin, Computer Uses in Education*, 1984, *18(1)*: 16-19.

Collins, R. *The Credential Society.* New York: Academic Press, 1980.

Conant, J. B. *The American High School Today.* New York: McGraw-Hill, 1959.

Cooper, C. and L. Odell (Eds.). *Research on Composing: Points of Departure.* Urbana, Illinois: National Council of Teachers of English, 1978.

Center for Social Organization of Schools. *School Uses of Microcomputers: Reports from a National Survey*, (1, 2), Baltimore, MD: The Johns Hopkins University, Center for the Organization of Schools, 1983.

Flavell, J. Monitoring the social-cognitive enterprise: something else that might develop in the area of social cognition. *Social Cognitive Development.* J. Flavell and L. Ross (Eds.). Cambridge: Cambridge University Press, 1981.

Florio-Ruane, S. and S. Dunn. Teaching writing: some perennial questions and some possible answers. *The Educator's Handbook.* V. Koehler (Ed.). New York: Longman, 1985.

Frank, M. *If You're Trying to Teach Kids How to Write, You've Gotta Have This Book!* Nashville: Incentive Publications, 1979.

Goodlad, J. I. *A Place Called School.* New York: McGraw-Hill, 1984.

Griffin, P. and M. Cole. Current activity for the future: the zo-ped. B. Rogoff and J. V. Wertsch (Eds.). *"Children's Learning in the Zone of Proximal Development." New Directions for Child Development.* No. 23, pp. 45-63. San Francisco: Jossey-Bass, 1984.

Hailey, J. *Teaching Writing, K through 8.* Berkeley: Professional Development and Applied Research Center, Department of Education, University of California, Berkeley, 1978.

Kulik, J. A., R. L. Bangert, and G. W. Williams. Effects of computer-based teaching on secondary school students. *Journal of Educational Psychology,* 1983, *75(1)*: 19-26.

Laboratory of Comparative Human Cognition, A model system for the study of learning disabilities. *The Quarterly Newsletter of the Laboratory of Comparative Human Cognition,* 1982, *4(3)*: 42-65.

Lesgold, A. When can computers make a difference? *Theory Into Practice,* 1983, *XXII(4)*: 247-252.

Levin, H. and R. Rumberger. The educational implications of high technology. Project Report #83-A4. Stanford: Stanford University, Institute for Research on Educational Finance and Governance, 1983.

Levin, J. A. Microcomputers as interactive communicative media: an interactive text interpreter. *The Quarterly Newsletter of the Laboratory of Comparative Human Cognition,* 1982, *4*: 34-36.

Levin, J. A., M. Boruta, and M. T. Vasconcellos. Microcomputer based environments for writing: a writer's assistant. A. C. Wilkinson (Ed.). *Classroom Computers and Cognitive Science.* New York: Academic Press, 1983.

Levin, J. A., M. Riel, M. Boruta, and R. Rowe. Muktuk meets jaccuzi: computer networks and elementary schools. Sarah Freedman (Ed.). *The Acquisition of Written Language.* New York: Ablex Publishing Company, 1984.

Levin, J. A. and R. Souviney. Computer literacy: a time for tools. *The Quarterly Newsletter of the Laboratory of Comparative Human Cognition,*

1983, *5*: 45-46.

Luria, A. R. *Cognitive Development.* Cambridge: Harvard University Press, 1976.

Malone, T. M. Toward a theory of intrinsic motivation. *Cognitive Science,* 1981, *4*: 335-369.

Marx, K. *Das Kapital.* New York: International Press, 1964.

Mehan, H., A. Hertweck, and J. L. Meihls. *Handicapping the Handicapped.* Stanford: Stanford University Press, 1985.

Mehan, H., B. Miller-Souviney, and M. M. Riel. Knowledge of text editing and the control of literacy skills. *Language Arts,* 1985, *(61)5*: 510-515.

Mehan, H., L. Moll, M. Riel, M. Boruta, C. Drale, N. Maroules, M. Tum Suden, A. Newcomb, and K. Whooley. Computers in classrooms: a quasi-experiment in guided change. (Final Report No. NIE-G-83-0027). Interactive Technology Laboratory (CHIP), University of California, San Diego, 1985.

Mehan, H. and H. Souviney (Eds.). *The Write Help: A Handbook for Computers in Classrooms.* Report No. 6. San Diego, CA: University of California, Interactive Technology Laboratory, 1984.

Miller, J. J. *Microcomputer Use in San Diego/Imperial County School Districts.* San Diego, CA: San Diego County Department of Education, 1983.

Miller-Souviney, B. Computer supported tools for expository writing: one teacher, twenty-eight kids. Unpublished M.A. Thesis, University of California, San Diego, 1985.

Newman, D. *Functional Learning Environments.* Technical Report #25. Center for Children and Technology. New York: Bank Street College of Education, 1984.

Ninio, A. and J. Bruner. The achievement and antecedents of labelling. *Journal of Child Language,* 1978, *5*: 5-15.

Papert, S. *Mindstorms.* Cambridge, MA: MIT Press, 1980.

Patterson, J. Theoretical secrets for intelligent software. *Theory Into Practice,* 1983, *XXII(4)*: 267-271.

Piaget, J. *Main Trends in Inter-Disciplinary Re-*

search. New York: Harper & Row, 1970.

Riel, M. M. Computer problem solving strategies and social skills of language impaired and normal children. Unpublished Ph.D. dissertation. University of California, Irvine, 1982.

Riel, M. Computer chronicles: a functional learning environment for literacy skills. *Journal of Education Computing Research*, 1983, *1(3)*: 3-24.

Riel, M. M., J. A. Levin, and B. Miller-Souviney. Dynamic support: interactive software development. Paper presented at AERA. New Orleans, LA: April 1984.

Schaff, J. *The New Language Arts Idea Book*. Glenview, IL: Scott, Foresman and Company, 1985.

Schiller, H. I. *Who Knows: Information in the Age of the Fortune 500*. Norwood, NJ: Ablex Publishing Company, 1981.

Sheingold, L., J. Kane, and M. Endreweit. Microcomputer use in schools. *Harvard Educational Review*, 1983, *53(4)*: 412-432.

Silberman, C. E. *Crisis in the Classroom*. New York: Vintage Books, 1970.

Suppes, P. The future of computers in education. R. P. Taylor (Ed.). *The Computer in the School*. New York: Teachers College Press, 1960.

Tiedt, I. M. *Teaching Writing in K-8 Classrooms: The Time Has Come*. Englewood Cliffs, NJ: Prentice-Hall, 1983.

Tucker, M. S. Computers in schools: a plan in time saves nine. *Theory Into Practice*, 1983, *22(4)*: 113-320.

Vygotsky, L. S. *Mind in Society: The development of higher psychological processes*. M. Cole, V. John-Steiner, S. Scribner, and E. Souberman (Eds.). Cambridge: Harvard University Press, 1978.

Welch, I. D. and S. E. Elliot. *A Year of Writing Activities*. New York: Scholastic Book Services, 1979.

Wertsch, J. V. From social interaction to higher psychological processes: a clarification and application of Vygotsky's theory. *Human Development*, 1979, *22*: 1-22.

Selected Software and Writing Resource Books

Software

Apple Presents Apple (Apple Computer). A simple tutorial introduction to the Apple IIe and IIc that describes the computer, the keyboard, and functions.

Apple Works (Apple Computer). Easy to use software which integrates word processing, data-base, and spreadsheet applications.

Apple Writer (Apple Computer). A professional-quality word processor; older children can use it for activities in this book which call for a word processor.

Bank Street Speller (Broderbund). A spelling verification program designed for use with *Bank Street Writer*.

Bank Street Writer (Broderbund). A word processing system developed specifically for young uers. It is designed for school use and includes tutorials and teaching applications.

CompuPoem (K-12 Micro-Media). A prompted writing environment for writing poetry; provides directions and advice for pre-writing experiences and composing of poems.

Computer Chronicles: The News Writing Tool (EBE Corp.). An interactive writing environment that helps students write different types of newspaper articles.

Expository Tool (EBE Corp.). An interactive writing environment that includes four activities to help students learn how to write expository compositions. The activities are arranged to provide more support at the beginning and less support as the students acquire skill.

Friendly Letter and *Business Letter Writing Tools* (EBE Corp.). A set of interactive texts which can be used to write specific types of friendly and business letters.

Interactive Text Interpreter—ITI (InterLearn). A special-purpose authoring system which can be used to create a range of interactive lessons, adventures, writing activities, questionaires, and forms.

Interactive Writing Tools (EBE Corp.). A set of ITI programs which provide dynamic support for the writing process. Students can be given the opportunity to select among options, read instructions, follow examples, or just receive encouragement. These simplified writing environments are used to create a first draft of text that later can be revised and edited with *The Writer's Assistant*.

The InterLearn Newswire Network (InterLearn). A subscription to a "newswire" in which students become reporters and editors. Reporters share their stories with other students on the network, and local editors make decisions about which newswire stories will be carried in their classroom edition of the *Computer Chronicles*.

Kids on Keys (Spinnaker Software). A program that helps students gain familiarity with the keyboard. It can be used as a typing or keyboard-familiarity exercise for one or more students.

MasterType (Scarborough Systems). An arcade game format for learning keyboard skills.

Narrative Writing Tool (EBE Corp.). Provides dynamic support for learning to write narrative compositions. The disk contains four programs which vary the level of support provided.

Poetry Writing Tool (EBE Corp.). An interactive writing environment that helps students write various forms of poetry, including haiku, limericks, diamante, and name poems.

QUILL (D.C. Heath). A set of programs which motivates students to employ a process approach to writing—i.e., pre-writing, revision, and editing. The set (which requires two disk drives and a printer) includes *The Writer's Assistant* word processor, the *Planner*, *Library*, and *Mailbag*.

QUILL Mailbag (D.C. Heath). The component of the *QUILL* set which serves as an electronic mail system for the classroom. Emphasizing communication as an important goal of writing, *Mailbag* makes it easy for students to send letters, memos, or invitations to anyone in the class.

QUILL Planners (D.C. Heath). The component of the *QUILL* set which helps writers generate and organize ideas by posing teacher-entered questions that suggest a plan for getting started. The text that is created is printed and used as a guide for writing. Since there is no provision for saving text on disk, however, the text created while using a *Planner* must be reentered.

Sensible Speller (Sensible Software). A spelling verification program. It contains over 80,000 words and is compatible with *The Writer's Assistant*.

Storymakers (Bolt, Berenak, and Newman). Interactive reading activities in which the students are asked to make selections among options. The created story is one of many possible versions. It is

not possible with this program to save the student's work on disk for editing.

Storytree (Scholastic). Allows students to select different story branches and thereby decide which way a story will unfold. Students can use a built-in word processor to write and edit storytrees, but there is no way to save the story that the student creates.

Typing Tutor III (Simon and Schuster). A program that helps students gain familiarity with the keyboard by doing typing exercises. It provides detailed graphic analysis of performance.

The Writer's Assistant (EBE Corp.). A word processing system that is adjustable for novice, intermediate, and advanced use. When the level of experience is set for novice, it functions as an entry-level word processor for elementary and secondary students. With the experience level set to intermediate or expert, it gives the user access to increasingly powerful functions that can reformat, transfer, find, and replace text.

WordStar (MicroPro International Corp.). A professional word processing program offering a wide range of features.

Writing Resource Books

Free Stuff For Kids (edited by Louise Delagran. Deephaven, MN: Meadowbrook Press, 1983). A comprehensive listing of addresses to which children can write for free information and items of interest.

Handbook for Planning an Effective Writing Program, Kindergarten Through Grade Twelve (by Handbook Writing Committee. California State Department of Education, Sacramento, CA: Department of Education, 1982; Computer Addendum, 1985). The California State Framework for developing a writing program provides a standard for assessing existing programs and a tool for designing new ones. It follows the stages of the writing process.

If You're Trying to Teach Kids How to Write, You've Gotta Have This Book! (by Marjorie Frank. Nashville, TN: Incentive Publications, 1979). A "must have" book for any grade level. Dealing not only with the "how" of writing but also with the problems associated with traditional writing programs in schools, it is written in a personal, easy-to-read style. The author covers topics from "My Kids Say They Can't Think of Anything to Write" to "How Can I Get Them to Write on Their Own?" In addition to a discussion of the writing process, the book includes many motivating, practical, ready-to-use ideas and activities.

In Your Own Words, A Beginner's Guide to Writing (by Sylvia Cassedy. Garden City, NY: Doubleday and Company, 1979). An approach to creative prose and poetry writing which emphasizes that writing starts with sensual awareness and perceptions. It contains excellent suggestions for teachers about where to begin and where to go from there.

The Kid's Whole Future Catalog (by Paula Taylor. New York: Random House, 1982). Filled with places to write for free or inexpensive brochures, pamphlets, books, and other interesting items.

Pathways to Imagination: Language Arts Learning Centers and Activities for Grades K-7 (by Angela S. Reeke and James L. Laffey. Glenview, IL: Scott, Foresman and Company, 1979). A book of language arts learning centers that can be utilized in the classroom. Writing activities are divided into categories (e.g., Creative Writing, Functional Writing, Library Skills, and Poetry). Each type of writing has a variety of ready-to-use activities with helpful diagrams of the centers.

Practical Guide to Computers in Education (by Peter Coburn, Peter Kelman, Nancy Roberts, Thomas Snyder, Daniel Watt, and Cheryl Weiner. Menlo Park, CA: Addison-Wesley Publishing Company, 1983). An excellent overview of computers and computing for the educator with little prior experience in the area.

Rose, Where Did You Get That Red? Teaching Great Poetry to Children (by Kenneth Koch. New York: Vintage Books, Random House, 1973). A handbook, anthology, and instructor's guide written by a poet who understands how to teach children in a way that moves them beyond "roses are red,

violets are blue."

Teaching Writing in K-8 Classrooms: The Time Has Come (by Tiedt, Bruemmer, Lane, Stelwagon, Watanabe, and Williams. Englewood Cliffs, NJ: Prentice-Hall, Inc., 1983). Written by Fellows of the South Bay Writing Project, this book explains different types of composition and provides step-by-step activities for instruction. Based on a "sequential holistic model that centers language arts instruction on composition," the book is useful for teaching different kinds of writing such as narrative and expository. It also includes methods for evaluating student work.

Teaching Writing K-8 (by Jack Hailey. Professional Development and Applied Research Center, Department of Education, University of California, Berkeley, 1978). A comprehensive overview of the writing process which deals with assessing students' work (holistic assessment) along with the teaching of writing. A discussion of the writing process is included along with ideas for "writing across the curriculum." Finally, the "Reviewing the Masters" section takes a look at the research end of writing and summarizes findings of some of the more noted researchers in the area of writing.

Wishes, Lies and Dreams, Teaching Children to Write Poetry (by Kenneth Koch. New York: Chelsea House Book, Harper & Row Publishers, 1970). Philosophical discussion of writing poetry and a guide to teaching children to write poetry. Discussion based on the author's own experience.

Write Here (by Joanne Richards and Marianne Standley. Nashville, TN: Incentive Publications, 1984). A series of writing activities that includes suggested motivation, story starters, materials, directions, and adaptations for cross-curricular applications. Suitable for grades 3-6.

Write Up A Storm, Creative Writing Ideas and Activities for the Middle Grades (by Linda Polon and Aileen Cantwell. Glenview, IL: Scott, Foresman and Company, 1979). Over 100 classroom-tested worksheets and activities that stimulate kids to use their imaginations to write. The activities, which can be easily adapted for computer writing, come from the children's own experiences and interests. Topics include "Tongue Twister Time," "Be an Abler Fabler," and "Produce Your Own Game Show."

The Writing Corner (by Arnold Cheyney. Glenview, IL: Scott, Foresman and Company, 1979). Full of information regarding the history of writing, creating the atmosphere for productive writing, as well as functional descriptions of different forms of writing such as poetry, short stories, reports, and essays. Included in this easy-to-read book are many practical "classroom-ready" ideas and a selection on "Creating the Classroom Newspaper." A section on "The Teacher Writes ... for Profit" may arouse interest among teacher/writers.

The Young Writer's Handbook, A Practical Guide for the Beginner Who Is Serious About Writing (by Susan and Stephen Tchudi. New York: Scribners, 1984). A well-constructed guide for young writers which offers ways to approach journal writing, fiction, plays, poems, news writing, editing, and publishing. An excellent resource for teachers and children.

Glossary

CENTRAL PROCESSING UNIT (CPU): The computer's brain—a complex electronic circuit which controls the processing of information inside the computer.

COMPUTER AIDED INSTRUCTION: A prevailing use of microcomputers in schools. Students are presented with a range of exercises in a predetermined order. Correct answers often generate positive reinforcement displays, while incorrect answers may produce a repetition of the exercise or a similar example. Based on the pattern of user responses, some corrective instruction may be employed, and the level of difficulty may be automatically adjusted.

DISK DRIVE: A mass storage device which records information on floppy disks.

DYNAMIC SUPPORT: The process of systematically reducing the amount of assistance provided to novices learning a task.

EVALUATION: The stage in the writing process in which peers and experts review the final product according to the original intent of the composition.

FLOPPY DISK: A flexible plastic disk which is commonly used to store text and other information for future use.

FUNCTIONAL LEARNING ENVIRONMENT: Learning situations which are organized for meaningful purposes rather than for evaluative purposes. Learning environments in language arts emphasize the communicative functions of language.

HOLISTIC EDUCATIONAL PRACTICE (THE WHOLE TASK): The organization of instruction so that students participate in whole activities with the support of others until they are capable of carrying out the entire task on their own.

INTERACTIVE CAPABILITIES OF COMPUTERS: An attribute of computers which enables users to share the initiative for modifying the learning situation while learning in a computer-supported environment.

INTERACTIVE WRITING TOOL: Writing software which exploits the interactive capabilities of computers.

KEYBOARD: A set of keys with symbols—positioned like those of a typewriter—used to input information into a computer.

MONITOR: A video device used in conjunction with the computer to communicate information to the user.

POST-WRITING: The final stage in the writing process during which compositions are shared, displayed, or published.

PRE-WRITING: The process of brainstorming and organizing ideas prior to writing.

PRINTER: A device used to make a "hard" (paper) copy of text or graphics.

RANDOM ACCESS MEMORY (RAM): Memory which temporarily stores information in the computer.

READ-ONLY MEMORY (ROM): Memory which contains information (e.g., BASIC language) that the computer uses frequently.

RESPONSE: The stage in the writing process during which writers get feedback about their compositions from peers and experts.

REVISION: Making corrections and other changes to create the final draft of a composition prior to evaluation.

SOFTWARE: Computer programs which cause a computer to carry out specified tasks.

TEXT DISK: A disk used exclusively for storing textfiles.

TEXTFILE: A computer file containing words or other symbols.

WORD PROCESSOR: A particular type of software that enables a computer to function somewhat like a typewriter, allowing the user to enter, edit, and print text.

WRITING: The act of composing the first draft of a story, poem, letter, or article.

WRITING PROCESS: The view that the composing process is made up of six interrelated steps—pre-writing, writing, response, revision, evaluation, and post-writing.

Appendix: Blackline Masters

WRITING WITH A PENCIL

To Write:

1. Move the PENCIL to the place you wish to write.

2. PUT THE LEAD POINT DOWN.

3. WRITE the words.

4. When finished, LIFT THE PENCIL.

To Erase:

1. Move the PENCIL to the spot you wish to erase.

2. PUT THE ERASER END DOWN.

3. Move the ERASER to remove the words.

4. When finished, LIFT THE PENCIL.

WRITING WITH A WORD PROCESSOR

To Write:

1. Move the CURSOR to the place where you want to write.

2. PRESS I FOR IN.

3. TYPE the words.

4. When finished, PRESS CTRL-C.

To Erase:

1. Move the CURSOR to the spot you wish to erase.

2. PRESS D FOR DROP.

3. Move the CURSOR over the words to be removed.

4. When finished, PRESS CTRL-C.

3

TYPING CENTER TASKS

a. type your name
b. type the names of your family
c. type the names of your classmates
d. type your address
e. type your telephone number
f. type the alphabet in lower case
g. type the alphabet in upper case
h. type numbers in sequence, 1 to 50
i. type a poem
j. type a riddle or a joke
k. type your spelling words
l. type your vocabulary list

TYPING CENTER

At this center you will practice your keyboarding skills.

— Turn the typewriter "on"

— Feed the paper into the machine

— Set your margins

— Choose an activity from the taskcard. Complete the activity

— Choose as many activities as you have time to do

— When the period is over:

    Clean up the center
    Put your work on display
    Turn the typewriter "off"

ROTATION SCHEDULE

	10:35 11:00	11:00 11:25	11:25 11:50	11:50 12:15
Red	Group	Seatwork	Centers	Writing
Yellow	Group	Writing	Seatwork	Centers
Green	Seatwork	Centers	Group	Writing
Blue	Centers	Writing	Group	Seatwork

CENTER SCHEDULE

	1 Computer	2 Library	3 Language	4 Listening
Julie		⊗		
Bud	⊗			
Barb			⊗	
Randy	⊗			
Kim				⊗
Steve		⊗		
Bea				⊗
Bob			⊗	

4 charts in different colors will accommodate 32 students in 4 groups of 8

⊗ indicates thumbtacks which are used to mark center assignment. Tacks are moved one space to the right each day. Partners may be changed from week to week.

APPLE ABILITY
Getting Started

— Select the disk with which you will be working. Carefully remove it from its jacket.

— Open the "garage door" of the disk drive and insert the disk, label up and "under your thumb. Close the "garage door."

— Turn on the MONITOR.

— Turn on the COMPUTER.

— Follow the directions on the screen.

— When you have finished, remove the disk, replace it in its jacket, store it in the box and turn the MONITOR and COMPUTER off.

From *The Write Help*, Copyright © 1986 Scott, Foresman and Company.

WHEN IN DOUBT
(Help Me! Help Me!)

If the computer is not doing as you think it should, try one of these <u>before</u> you call a computer tutor or a teacher.

- Is it plugged in?
- Is it turned on?
- Is the monitor on?
- Did you push RETURN?
- Did you push CONTROL-C?
- Did you <u>read</u> the screen for further directions?

If you can answer, "yes," to all of these questions and you still can't get results...

CALL COMPUTER TUTOR

GET ME OUT OF HERE

If you need to "get out" of a program or back to the beginning, try these in order.

- Push **ESC**
- Push **Q**
- Push **CONTROL & RESET**
- Push **PR # 6**

NO LUCK ?

CALL
COMPUTER TUTOR

Warning! **DO NOT** turn the computer off

NAMING IT

How to label a piece of writing before saving it :

Prompt : TEXT NAME ▨ ▨

Input : J - O 27 - MP

Name Code *

first letter of month

Date

Kind of Writing *

RETURN

* Naming Code List

NAMING CODES

1	Karen
2	Tim
3	Michelle
4	Bud
5	Margaret
6	Randy
7	Barbara
8	Bea
9	Luis
A	Bobbie
B	Marty
C	Christie
D	Cyndy
E	Gloria
F	Steve
G	Marcia
H	Jim
I	Michael
J	Megan
K	Kim

L	Chelsea
M	Linda
N	Rahn
O	Cheri
P	Will
Q	Norma
R	Isabel
S	Kathy
T	
U	
V	
W	
X	
Y	
Z	

Kind of Writing

MP- Monster Poem
SS - Silly Sentences
AA - Animal Antics
SW - Star Wars
CP - Computer Pals
EW- Expository Writing

<u>SAVING</u> <u>IT</u>

How to save what you have written on a

WA-TEXT: disk

- <u>After</u> you have named your text, remove the Interactive Text Tool disk from the disk drive

- Place WA-TEXT: disk in disk drive

- Push RETURN ... the drive will "spin" and the light will go on

- When the light goes out, remove the WA-TEXT: disk

- You may write again by replacing the Interactive Text Tool

13

FINDING IT

How to find something you have saved on a TEXT disk

- Boot WA-SYS:disk, select option #1, push RETURN

- Follow screen directions:
  You will be directed to remove WA-SYS:disk, insert WA-TEXT:, then push L

- If you do not remember the code for your text, push SHIFT ? RETURN and select the text from the list provided. Push the label letter next to your text and RETURN

- If you do remember the code, enter it and push RETURN

PRESTO, CHANGO!
There's your text

From *The Write Help*, Copyright © 1986 Scott, Foresman and Company.

CURSOR MOVEMENT CHART

SPACE (moving right)   ↑ (moving up)

RETURN (moving to next line)   ↓ (moving down)

→ (moving right)   O (moving up)

← (moving left)   L (moving down)

CURSOR MOVEMENT TASKS

a. Move the cursor over the first letter in the text, then to the last letter in the text

b. Move the cursor up 5 lines, then down 3 lines, then 4 words to the right.

c. Move the cursor to the first <u>noun</u> in the text, then to the last <u>adjective</u> in the text.

d. Move the cursor as quickly as possible to the last period in the text.

EDITING COMMAND CHART

I – to type **I**n text
D – to **D**rop letters and words
Q – to **Q**uit after writing
U – to **U**pdate text on the disk
CONTROL-C – to "freeze" or
lock in text after using
In or **D**rop

OPENING SCREEN DISPLAYS

```
                    ****************************************

                              Welcome to

                       the Writer's Assistant System.

                    ****************************************
```

```
                 Choose (1, 2, 3, or 4)
                  then push  RETURN.



          ->1) The Writer's Assistant
                  For writing and revising texts
            2) The Printing Press
                  For printing the text files
            3) The File Cabinet
                  For organizing files on your disk
            4) The Initializer
                  For preparing brand-new disks



                 (c) 1985 InterLearn Inc
            Box 342, Cardiff by the Sea, CA  92007
                Portions (c) 1978 Regents
             University of California, San Diego
```

```
  To return to the List of tools, push  L.
         ------


  *****************************************
  *                                       *
  *    To write or edit text:             *
  *                                       *
  *  - First put in your                  *
  *    Writer's Assistant Text Disk       *
  *                                       *
  *  - Then push  L                       *
  *                                       *
  *****************************************
```

```
  >The Writer's Assistant

  Hi, who are you?




                 (c) 1985
       InterLearn Inc, Box 342 Cardiff CA 92007
               Portions (c) 1978
       The Regents of University of California,
                  San Diego
```

FOR THE WRITER'S ASSISTANT

```
>The Writer's Assistant




What text do you want
 to work on?



    Push  ?  to see the available texts.
```

```
>W:In / Drop / Quit / Help /  ?
==========================================
```

```
>Quit

Choose one of the following:

U  to save TEST.TEXT
     and leave

S  to save TEST.TEXT
     and return to your text

E  to exit without saving your text

R  to return to your text without saving

W  to save your text under a new name

A  to save TEST.TEXT
     and work on another text
```

```
>Quit

Print a draft of this text?
```

FRIENDLY LETTER

May 15, 1986 **(date)**

(greeting) Dear Computer Pal,

(body)
    My name is Russell and I am a cat. I have long
orange and white fur. My paws and belly are white.
I weigh 17 pounds in the winter and 14 pounds in
the summer. I shed my fur (and some fat). I was
born in a foreign country, named Papua New Guinea.
My owner tries to spoil me by letting me do my
two favorite things, eating and sleeping. I also
chase birds. I HATE dogs. I lead a very carefree
life on the roof of our house in California, and I
am glad that I was born to be who I am.

    I would love to find out about you. What is
your name and what do you look like? Where do
you live and what are your favorite free-time
activities? Who takes care of you? Are you
happy? Please write back and tell me about
yourself. I am looking forward to your reply.

(closing) Your Friend,

Russell

(signature) Russell

FRIENDLY LETTER
TASK CARD

Make these changes in FRIENDLY.TEXT

a. Change the year in the date to the year you were born.

b. Change the name in the greeting to the name of your best friend.

c. Change one of the places mentioned in the letter to one you have visited.

d. Add a question to the ending of the letter.

e. Write a new closing.

f. Change the name to your name.

20

COMPUTER PAL TASK CARD

When writing a Computer Pal Letter:
a. Describe yourself (color of hair, eyes, skin, etc.).
b. Describe your interests (school, hobbies, etc.).
c. Describe your family (include pets).
d. Ask questions about your computer pal.

From *The Write Help,* Copyright © 1986 Scott, Foresman and Company.

BUSINESS LETTER

Lion Obedience School
100 Park Avenue
San Diego, CA 92093
USA
February 12, 1986

(inside address)

Whiskas Cat Food Company
14876 Feline Avenue
Sydney, New South Wales
Australia 6447

(greeting) Dear Sir:

(body)
   While I was living in Papua New Guinea a few years back, I regularly enjoyed your brand of canned cuisine imported from Australia. I looked forward to many years of pleasant dining until one day my owner packed me in a small cage and flew me to California to live. Ever since my arrival, I have been yearning for a can of your rare and wonderful food, but I can't find it anywhere. My owner tries to convince me to accept a substitute "generic brand" cat food, but I continue to hold out for the "original."

   Can you help me please? Do you have an importer for your products in this country? Please forward a list of suppliers in my area. Your quick and speedy reply will be much appreciated.

(closing) Sincerely,

Russell

(signature) Russell

22

BUSINESS LETTER
TASK CARD

Make the following changes in BUSINESS.TEXT:

a. Change the date in the heading to the current date.

b. Change the inside address to our school's address.

c. Change the name in the greeting to your teacher's.

d. Replace "quick" and "speedy" in the last line to two antonyms for those words.

e. Insert a new closing.

f. Change the signature to your name.

REQUEST LETTER CHART

- State your reasons for wanting certain items offered by the company, (I am studying about pets and would like your free booklet on Pet Care).

- Include the address where items should be sent if it is different than the address in the heading of the letter.

- Be sure to thank the company ahead of time for sending the materials.

ADDRESSING AN ENVELOPE

2839 Sebastian
Cardiff, CA 92007 (Return Address)

(Address)

Ms. Computer Pal
64 K Ram Ram St.
Appletown, CA
6502

22¢

HAIKU POETRY

A Haiku expresses a <u>thought</u>, a <u>feeling</u>, or an <u>observation</u> about nature.

It has no rhyme. It has 3 lines.

Line <u>1</u> -- 5 syllables
Line <u>2</u> -- 7 syllables
Line <u>3</u> -- 5 syllables

For example:

The Sun is so bright
Shining on the earth all day
Till the day is done.

EXPOSITORY COMPOSITION

1. <u>TITLE</u> — Name for your composition

2. <u>BY</u> — Type your name

3. <u>INTRODUCTORY PARAGRAPH</u> —
   "<u>Main Idea</u>"
   Tell why you are writing about it

4. <u>BODY</u> — Give details of your "Main Idea" Give step by step instructions of how to do it <u>in</u> <u>order</u>

5. <u>CONCLUSION</u> — Tell how you feel when you finish the activity or when you will do it again

NEWS CENTER

- Select an article which interests you from the scrapbook.

- Read the article very carefully.

- Write a summary without looking at it again. Remember
    WHO ?   WHERE ?
    WHAT?   WHEN ?
    WHY ?
If you can't remember, look again !

- Write a comment or opinion about the article. What do you think?

- Find the location of the event on the wall map. Label it on the small map.

- Staple the map to your summary. Put your completed paper in the folder for others to read.

- Read what others have written. Read the scrapbook.

From *The Write Help*, Copyright © 1986 Scott, Foresman and Company.

COMPUTER CHRONICLES:
NEWS WRITING TOOL

Garrison Bureau

Welcome Cub Reporters!

This week is get acquainted week. These directions will help you to use the Computer Chronicles: News Writing Tool disk and let you practice storing text for future editing. Enjoy the exploration and experimentation!

The Field Editor

COMPUTER CHRONICLES: NEWS WRITING TOOL

▪ DIRECTIONS ▪

- ▪ Boot Computer Chronicles: News Writing Tool.

- ▪ Follow instructions on screen.

- ▪ Select the section for which you wish to write. Enter your text.

- ▪ Five minutes before the end of the period, STOP writing.

- ▪ SAVE what you have written on the disk labeled "WA-TEXT: for saving stories."

- ▪ PRINT 2 copies. Make sure your names are on the printout. File them in the folders.

EDITING CODES

∧   (caret) means something has been left out

Ø   slash through a capital letter means make it lower case

r̲̲̲   three lines under a lower case letter means make it a capital

(sp)   circled sp above a word means the word is misspelled

₱   double lined P means make a new paragraph

✳   (asterisk) means to look at the note at the bottom of the page

EDITING CHECKLIST

1. Does your topic sentence tell what the paragraph is about?

2. Do the rest of the sentences give details about the main idea?

3. Does each sentence express a complete idea?

4. Did you indent at the beginning of each paragraph?

5. Did you capitalize all proper nouns and the first word of each sentence?

6. Does each sentence end with the proper punctuation mark?

7. Did you use proper punctuation <u>in</u> each sentence?

8. Did you check spelling?

EDITING
COMPUTER CHRONICLES

To finish or edit an article:

- Boot the WA-SYS: disk.

- Select option 1.

- Insert TEXT disk on which you previously stored article.

- Follow screen directions and those for FINDING IT.

- Edit text using I and D commands as before.

- Be careful to save time to QUIT, UPDATE and print 2 copies for the file folders.

Notes

Notes

Notes